As They
See Us

Walter Stewart

AS THEY SEE US

McClelland and Stewart

ISBN: 0-7710-8354-8

The Canadian Publishers
McClelland and Stewart Limited
25 Hollinger Road, Toronto M4B 3G2

Printed and bound in Canada

Illustrations by Al King

For Joan,
who drove
me to it

Contents

As They
See Us

Introduction

There is no American attitude to Canada. Some Americans love us, some despise us, most view us with indifference. Sometimes, the indifference is tinged with contempt; more often, with warmth. Sometimes it contains neither heat nor cold, it is indifference pure and simple. No generalizations hold up. It cannot be shown that the average American – whoever he or she may be – likes us or doesn't, respects us or doesn't, finds us amusing, or just doesn't give a damn. The attitude of any given American towards Canada depends entirely on his own association – or lack of it – with Canadians. Americans are not constantly confronted, as we are, with the actions and neglects, comings and goings, virtues and failures, of their next-door neighbour. We, perforce, hold strong views about them because they loom across our horizon, dominate our trade, bestride our culture; we love them or we hate them, but we are not indifferent. They can afford a wider range of responses. For most of them, we are merely a background noise; it is easy to tune us out.

So, the first finding from the hundreds of interviews that make up this book is that I have spent twenty months on a wild goose chase – or, more romantically, seeking a Holy Grail. I have been trying to discover what Americans really think about us, only to find that the question has no single answer. Just the same, I found the quest a useful one – Sir Gawain, I remember, felt the same way about his Holy Grail – because I have learned a great deal, been delighted, perplexed, astounded, amused, and outraged along the way. I trust that any reader who follows me will experience similar emotions.

I began collecting the material for this book in October 1974, while my family and I were still living in Toronto, and took a month-long trip across the US to San Francisco. Then, in June 1975, we moved to Washington, and subsequently took two more month-long cross-country auto swings and a score of lesser rambles fanning out from the US capital – to Pittsburgh, Mobile, New York, Boston, Philadelphia, Williamsburg, Miami, Newark and Bangor, Maine. These quotes, then, were gathered over a period of twenty months from late 1974 to summer 1976.

The surveying technique was not scientific, nor even consistent: By not scientific, I mean that no attempt was made to balance the sample for race, economic level, religion, urban-vs-rural background, or even sex. I simply lighted on whomever happened to be handy and blurted out my question: What do you think of when you think of Canada or Canadians? By not consistent, I mean that the question wasn't always put that way. It depended on how the conversation got started. Sometimes we would get to talking about other things – the weather, the road, the Liberty Bell (in Philadelphia) – and I would lead the talk around to Canada.

At first, I always carried my tape recorder at the ready, sometimes I even had it on as I strolled along. That is how I picked up the remarkable exchange with a Washington prostitute, that appears on p. 42. But a tape recorder can be inhibiting, even to a people as accustomed to being badgered, surveyed, and poked at with hidden cameras as the Americans. In a small town in Alabama I braced the local police force in a dry goods store, hoisted up my tape recorder, and asked him what he thought of Canada. He began to make abrupt gestures with his hand, but didn't say anything. Finally, he made a cutting motion, and it dawned on me that he wanted me to turn the tape recorder off. I did that, and he said, "Try to tape me, boy, and ah'll break your arm." I said, "Oh." After that, I was more circumspect; sometimes I used the recorder, sometimes not. I always carried a notebook, and turned to that if the subject seemed likely to balk.

I laid out a little line of patter at the beginning of every interview; I said I was a Canadian journalist plumbing American views of Canada, that I was anxious to include the views of someone as obviously plugged full of wisdom as the subject before me, and then I launched my question. After a time, it occurred to me that I was loading the question without meaning to; when I announced that I was a Canadian, politeness overwhelmed frankness, which explained the overwhelmingly favourable comments I was hearing. So I stopped saying I was a Canadian and just said I was doing "research." Good word, research, it sounds scholarly, not like asking a lot of dumb questions.

I also dropped my earlier resolve to use everybody's name, age, and address, the way I was taught as a boy journalist many years ago. People who thought they might be held to account some day, might be criticized, or even singled out, either clammed up or retreated into banalities. Knowing they were free to fire away, my subjects began to put a little more muscle into their remarks. I was astonished to find that – particularly in the US civil service – there are pockets of entrenched ill-feeling towards Canada, once the discussion is opened to uninhibited comment.

Criticisms of us, of our doings and character, tend to be specific, nearly always linked to the speaker's own particular interest: criticism of Medicare by a doctor, for example; of beef marketing by a farmer, or energy policy by oilmen. Favourable comments tend to be vaguer in tone – we are a peaceable, pastoral and pleasant people in the view of a great many Americans who know very little about us. In fact, a more careful scientist than myself could, I think, find a direct relationship between knowledge and hostility, kindliness and ignorance. To know us is not to love us; the civil servants, businessmen and professionals who have reason to know something about Canada because they deal with us directly are often scathing, while the nice folks in Alabama or California, Texas or Colorado, know little about us, and find us admirable. I suspect this law of benign ignorance applies to all countries, not just Canada and the US.

To put today's comments in context, I have rounded up earlier remarks about us, which are chiefly remarkable for the belligerence with which we have been regarded – popular myth to the contrary – over much of American history. These comments have been interspersed among the modern remarks to suggest parallels in the themes of American attitudes toward us that go back a long way. We, and our land, have been despised, disliked, or lusted after far more often than we have been embraced by the US. The cliché-ridden undefended border is a phenomenon of comparatively modern times.

I have edited some quotations, but not much; the three dots . . . indicate where I have taken something out.

Finally, I have used only about half the quotes gathered, since so many of the themes, and even the words, tended to repeat themselves. I accept no responsibility for the views propounded; the ignorance often appalled me, the occasional hostility astonished me, and some of the offbeat comments – that Canadians sleep a lot, for example, or that we can't cook – struck me as simply daffy. I do accept responsibility for trying to depict, fairly and accurately, the complex range of American views about Canada.

Washington, July 1976

Harsh Words and Honeyed Ones: 1774-1812

Canadian-American relations began even before there was a USA, with numerous petitions from the Continental Congresses to the people of Canada – mainly the French-speaking inhabitants of what is now Quebec. Optimistic Americans hoped that our ancestors would leap to the barricades and join the rebellious colonies in throwing off the hated English yoke. Pessimists, who turned out to have the right dope, thought it unlikely, but hoped at least that the Canadians would not join the British forces ranged against them. As a result, the early American comments about our nation consisted of lashings of flattery mixed with veiled threats. After the Revolutionary War, the Americans were too busy sorting out their own affairs to give us much attention, although there were a number of squabbles about the border; but with the build-up of tensions that led to the War of 1812, they made it clear that they could lick us, and expected to, at any time. When war broke out, they were sure that the capture of Canada was merely a matter of marching.

October, 1774: Invitation to the Dance
The power of making laws for you is lodged in the governor and council, all of them dependent upon and removable at the pleasure of a minister. . . .Have not Canadians sense enough to attend to any public affairs, than gathering stones from one place and piling them in another? Unhappy people! Who are not only injured but insulted. Nay more! With such superlative contempt for your understanding and spirit has an insolent ministry presumed to think of you, our respectable fellow-subjects, to take up arms, and render you the ridicule and detestation of the world, by becoming tools in their hands to assist them in taking that freedom from us, which they have treacherously denied to you. . . .We do not ask you, by this address, to commence hostilities against the government of your common sovereign. We only invite you to consult your own glory and welfare. . . .and elect deputies who after meeting

16

in a provincial congress, may choose delegates to represent your province in the Continental Congress to be held at Philadelphia on the Tenth of May, 1775.

Manifesto to the People of Quebec,
from the First Continental Congress

May 29, 1775: A Dash of Pity And A Soupçon of Contempt
Since the conclusion of the late war, we have been happy in considering you as fellow-subjects, and from the commencement of the present plan for subjugating the continent, we have viewed you as fellow-sufferers with us. . .

We most sincerely condole with you on the arrival of that day, in the course of which the sun could not shine on a single freeman in all your extensive dominion. Be assured, that your unmerited degradation has engaged the most unfeigned pity of your sister colonies; and we flatter ourselves you will not, by tamely bearing the yoke, suffer that pity to be supplanted by contempt. . . .By the introduction of your present form of government, or rather present form of tyranny, you and your wives are made slaves. You have nothing that you can call your own, and all the fruits of your labour and industry may be taken from you, whenever an avaritious [sic] governor and a rapacious council may be inclined to demand them. . . .You are liable by their edicts to be transported into foreign countries to fight battles in which you have no interest, and to spill your blood in conflicts from which neither honour nor emolument can be derived: Nay, the enjoyment of your very religion, in the present system, depends on a legislature in which you have no share, and over which you have no control, and your priests are exposed to expulsion, banishment, and ruin, whenever their wealth and possessions furnish sufficient temptation. . . .

It cannot be presumed that these considerations will have no weight with you, or that you are so lost to all sense of honour. We can never believe that the present race of Canadians are so degenerate as to possess neither the spirit, the gallantry, nor the courage of their ancestors . . . .

As our concern for your welfare entitles us to your friendship, we presume you will not, by doing us injury, reduce us to the disagreeable necessity of treating you as enemies.

Address of the Continental Congress to
the Oppressed Inhabitants of Canada,
May 29, 1775

September, 1775: Promises, Promises
We shall hold [Canadian] rights as dear as our own, and on their union with us, exert our utmost endeavours to obtain for them and their posterity the blessings of a free government.

John Hancock, speaking to the Second
Continental Congress

November 14, 1775: Give Up, Quebec

The American Congress, induced by motives of humanity, have at their request sent Gen. Schulyer into Canada for their relief. To cooperate with him, I am ordered by His Excellency, Gen. Washington, to take possession of the town of Quebec. I do, therefore, in the name of the United Colonies, demand surrender of the town, fortifications, etc., of Quebec to the forces of the United Colonies under my command; forbidding you to injure any of the inhabitants of the town in their person or property, as you will answer to the same at your peril. On surrendering the town the property of every individual shall be secured to him; but if I am obliged to carry the town by storm, you may expect every severity practised on such occasions.

General Benedict Arnold in a letter to
the Lieutenant Governor of Quebec

December 6, 1775: I Said, Give Up, Quebec!

You have a great extent of works from their nature incapable of defence, manned by a motley crew of sailors, the greatest part our friends, or of citizens who wish to see us within their walls, and a few of the worst troops ever to style themselves soldiers.

General Richard Montgomery to Governor
Guy Carleton, outside Quebec

January, 1776: Aw, Come On, Fellas, Give Up!
The Unanimous Voice of the Continent is Canada must be ours; Quebec must be taken.

John Adams, in a statement on the death
of General Montgomery in the abortive
attack on Quebec, New Year's Day, 1776.
Adams went on to become president; Quebec
went on untaken.

A PERTINENT QUESTION.

MRS. BRITANNIA.—"IS IT POSSIBLE, MY DEAR, THAT YOU HAVE EVER GIVEN YOUR COUSIN JONATHAN ANY ENCOURAGEMENT?"

MISS CANADA.—"ENCOURAGEMENT! CERTAINLY NOT, MAMMA. I HAVE TOLD HIM WE CAN *NEVER* BE UNITED."

from A Caricature History
of Canadian Politics,
published by Peter Martin
Associates Limited

1777: Oh, Well, If You Feel That Way . . .
Canada, acceding to the Confederation and joining in the measure of the United States, shall be admitted into, and entitled to all the advantages of Union.

from the Articles of Confederation
of the Thirteen Colonies

1778: Let Me Make One Thing Perfectly Clear
If the United States should think fit to attempt the reduction of the British power, remaining in the Northern parts of America, or the islands of the Bermudas, those countries or islands, in case of success, shall be confederated with or dependent upon the said United States.

Article V, A Treaty of Alliance
between the US and France

1778: The Whole Thing
No pent-up Utica contracts your powers, but the whole boundless continent is yours.

Jonathan Mitchell Sewall, Revolutionary
War slogan

November 1, 1784: Let's Subvert the Rascals
In the meantime the acquistion of Canada is not an object with us, we must make valuable what we have already acquired and at the same time take such measures as to weaken it as a British province.

James Monroe, in a letter to Thomas
Jefferson, before either became president

1810: After A Pause, A New Round of Bluster
It is absurd to suppose that we will not succeed. We have the Canadians as much under our command as Great Britain has the ocean, and the way to conquer her on the ocean is to drive her from the land. I am not for stopping at Quebec or anywhere else; but I could take the whole continent from her and ask no favours. I wish never to see peace till we do. God has given us the power and the means. We are to blame if we do not use them . . . The conquest of Canada is within your

power. I trust I shall not be presumed presumptuous when I state, what I verily believe, that the militia of Kentucky alone are competent to place Montreal and Upper Canada at your feet. Is it nothing to the British nation – is it nothing to the pride of her monarch to have the last of the immense North American possessions held by him in the commencement of his reign wrested from his dominion? . . Is it nothing to acquire the entire fur trade connected with that country and to destroy the temptation and opportunity of violating your revenue and other laws?

Senator Henry Clay of Kentucky, in debate

1811: Wanted: One Liberator, Good Condition

Were five thousand men to be sent into the Province with the Proclamation of Independence, the great mass of the people would join the American government.

John Mellish, American visitor to Canada

1812: Have Guns, Will Travel

Should the conquest of Canada be resolved, how pleasing the prospect that would open to the young volunteer, while performing a military promenade into a distant country. A succession of new and interesting objects would perpetually fill and delight his imagination, the effect of which would be heightened by the warlike appearances, the martial music, and the grand evolutions of an army of fifty thousand men. But why should these inducements be held out to the young men of America? They need them not, animated as they are to rival the exploits of Rome, they will never prefer an inglorious sloth, a supine inactivity to the honourable toil of carrying the Republican standard to the Heights of Abraham.

Andrew Jackson, later president

1812: Look Ma, No Soldiers

We can take Canada without soldiers! We have only to send officers into the Provinces, and the people, already disaffected toward their own government, will rally to our standard.

William Eustis, Secretary of War

June, 1812: Good Old Dan

A large portion of the people believe that a desire for the conquest and final retention of Canada is the mainspring of public measures . . . You are, you say, at war for maritime rights, and free trade. But they see you lock up your commerce and abandon the ocean. They see you invade an interior province of the enemy. They see you involve yourselves in a bloody war with the native savages; and they ask if you have, in truth, a maritime controversy with the Western Indians, and are really contending for sailors' rights with the tribes of the Prophet.

> *Representative (later Senator) Daniel Webster,*
> *speaking against the war in the House*
> *of Representatives*

July 12, 1812: Last Chance, Guys, Give Up?

The army under my command has now invaded your country . . . Separated by an immense ocean and an extensive wilderness from Great Britain, you have no participation in her councils, nor interest in her conduct. You have felt her tyranny; you have seen her injustice . . . Many of your fathers fought for the freedom and independence we now enjoy. Being children, therefore, of the same family with us, and heirs of the same heritage, the arrival of an army of friends must be hailed by you with a cordial welcome . . . If the barbarous and savage policy of Great Britain be pursued, and the savages are let loose to murder our citizens, and murder our women and children, this war will be a war of extermination. The first strike of the tomahawk, the first attempt with the scalping knife, will be the signal of one indiscriminate scene of desolation. No white man found fighting by the side of an Indian will be taken prisoner – instant death will be his lot.

> *General William Hull, Appeal to the*
> *Inhabitants of Canada*

August 4, 1812: It Was A Hell of a Long March

The acquisition of Canada this year, as far as the neighbourhood of Quebec, will be a mere matter of marching.

> *Thomas Jefferson, in a letter. He was no*
> *longer president when he wrote this, so*
> *it was all right to be wrong.*

The Queen, Bless Her

She Always Says, "Please"
That's a very fine place, with very fine people, but they've still got a Queen up there tells them what to do. I wouldn't like that if I was them.
Warehouse clerk, Providence, Rhode Island

Oh, Yeah, Everybody Says The Post Office Is Great
We lived in Canada for a while, and let me tell you, it was better than this. You didn't get long lines everywhere you went. You didn't have to wait in a long line and then when you got there they would close the window on you, like here. The post office of Canada is a lot better. It's kind of a reassuring place, they have a picture of the Queen and everything. They say Royalty is bad, and to tell you the truth, Canadians themselves aren't so hot on it; but if you ask me, it's better than what we've got here.
Disgruntled patron in a post office line-up,
Chevy Chase, Maryland

The Essentials
The only thing I know about Canada was what we were taught in school, which wasn't much. Something about the Queen and King, I remember that. As a matter of fact, I don't know a damn thing about Canada.
Police officer, McAlister, Alabama

No, No, First The President, Then The Queen, Then The USA
We're taught a great respect for Canada, we regard Canada as our ally above all. Canada isn't as loyal as it pretends to be to the Crown, that's all old stuff today. Canadians think a lot more of the USA than they do of the Queen.

Industrial engineer, Nederland, Colorado

It's Called A Constitutional Monarchy
What kind of a country still has a Queen these days? When she says squat, they squat? Canada is okay, I got nothing against them; but I don't understand how they can still go along with Great Britain, a country that is going straight down the drain, thanks to the fact that it's got a Queen. And another thing, do they have the nobility up there, dukes and that? Because if they do, that's really dumb; that's why we kicked the British out in the first place.

Short order cook, New York City

Political Science Lesson
You know what I really like? The Queen. Canada still has a Queen. I really like that. Here, the head of state is the president, and he's in charge. That puts him in an impossible position, he's supposed to be above politics, but everything he does is political, anyone can see that. Canada has the perfect way out – a Queen. They can pay her homage, she can be the centre of ceremonies, she can embody the nation, or what it wants to stand for, but she hasn't got a damn thing to do with the price of butter and who got laid off last week. We could learn something there, but I doubt if we will.

Teacher, Des Moines, Iowa

Royal, too
The Queen represents everything that is decent and traditional.

Business executive, Philadelphia

Wanted: One Monarch

We should have something like that to look up to. They don't
have to be smart, or do anything. They just have to be there.
  Housewife, Washington, DC

Well, A Boat's Better Than Nothing

We were here about two hours. More than two hours, I guess,
waiting to see her. It was a terrific thrill when she stepped
ashore [from the Royal Yacht Britannia] . . . I didn't actually
see the Queen, no, but I saw the boat.
  *Retired librarian, Baltimore, on the docks at Philadelphia
  for Her Majesty's arrival to begin her Bicentennial visit*

And 'Ray For You, Too, Fella

It's great to be an American, but 'ray for the Queen.
  *Chant from the crowd outside Independence Hall,
  Philadelphia, during the royal visit*

The People

Z-z-z-z

Canadians sleep all the time. They sleep more than any other people in the whole, wide world. Every time you turn around, they're going off somewhere to have a nap.

Printer, Huntington, New York

A Nation of What?

Canadians have been trying to have it both ways for far too long. Take this matter of the draft dodgers. We had draft dodgers pouring out of this country by the thousand, by the thousand. I read someplace that there were more than ten thousand draft dodgers in Toronto alone. And what did Canada do? It got up on its hind legs, is what, and said the draft dodgers was none of its business. Well, I lost a boy in Vietnam, he was blown up by a goddamn booby-trap, and I take it hard when somebody says that my boy can be killed but if some other yellow-belly wants to run off and refuse to fight, why, that's all right with them. I've never been to Canada and I never want to go; as far as I'm concerned, it's just a nation of assholes.

Independent businessman, Mobile, Alabama

Nice Folks
They're nice folks, not in a hurry all the time. They're like southerners in that, though, of course, they live up north.

Farm wife, near Evergreen, Alabama

Time for Each Other
The pace is slower, that's what I like. People have time for each other, not like here. And crime, there isn't so much. I read that in Canada, the police don't even carry guns. Or was that England? Anyway, people in Canada don't spend their time going around blowing each other up and stabbing each other and shooting each other and putting bombs in a guy's car, which is what people around here spend their time doing.

Druggist, Detroit

The Drivers Are Crazy
Canadian drivers are crazy. I'm sorry but there's no other word for it. They put their foot on the gas and their hand on the horn and look out, here I come. I wonder if it's got anything to do with their religion.

Tour guide, Williamsburg, Virginia

Stubborn Citizen
I got a friend comes from Canada, he lived just the other side of the river from Detroit, a place called Ottawa, I believe it was. We were in the service together and I brought him down here afterwards and introduced him to a girl and he married her. Now he refuses to give up his Canadian citizenship. Every year he goes up to Canada and gets a piece of paper, so he's still a Canadian citizen. This has been going on for six, seven years. I don't think you'd see an American do a thing like that. Strange.

Gas station attendant, Greensboro, North Carolina

Lawd, Yes
A God-fearing people, instilled and inspired of the true love of Jesus, an example to others, as the Book says.

Lay preacher, Racine, Wisconsin

Old Folks and Young Punks

Well, you don't see such a good quality of Canadians down here as you might somewhere else, that's my guess, anyway. We get two kinds of them, mostly – old folks and young punks. You see the young punks swarming around on spring break; they're up and down the beaches, drinking beer, screwing around, getting drunk, throwing up, fighting, stuff like that. Dope, too, lots of it. Don't give me that crap Canadian kids are any better or different or clean cut; they're just a bunch of punks like the American kids you see doing the same things. Kids, Christ, they're all spoiled rotten now, ain't they? So that's one, the punks. The old folks, they aren't so bad. They come down here to retire, or spend the winter away from all that snow. Some of them are quiet, kind of, some of them are always kicking up a stink about something or other, the prices or the service or what's the matter with America, anyway? I got to admit that pisses me off some, people come down here from some place like Montreal, which, if you ask me, from what I read in the papers it's got plenty of troubles of its own, and start bitching about the way we do things down here. I'm not saying everything is perfect by a long shot, but if they don't like it here, why don't they go home? Because it's too damn cold, I guess.

Restaurant manager, Miami, Florida

Oh, Shoot

They're dependent, the people, they don't stick up for themselves, the way people do here. The Second Amendment is very important here, it's part of our life. In Canada, they just holler for a cop whenever they get into trouble.

Engineer, Arlington, Virginia (The Second Amendment to the US Constitution reads "A well-regulated militia being necessary to the security of a free State, the right of the people to keep and bear arms shall not be infringed." Usually only the last part is quoted.)

Spiritual Us
Canadians are more spiritual than Americans.
Book store clerk, New York City

Turn Left At The Beaver And Keep Going
Canada? I don't know nothing about it. This bus just goes to
Farragut Square.
Bus driver, Washington, DC

Style Note
They wear their hats funny. My wife's cousin, she's going with
a Canadian boy, and he come over to dinner one night. Wore
his hat up, right up there on the top of his head, didn't pull it
down or nothing. An American wears a hat, he's going to pull
it down where it does some good. This was a winter hat, muffs
for the ears, it was cold, but he didn't even have the muffs
pulled down. I guess Canadians are used to that, the cold. Else
this boy wasn't very smart.
Security Guard, Library of Congress, Washington, DC

And the Farmers, of Course, are City Slickers
The city people in Canada are pretty much like the farm people
in this country.
Student, University of New Mexico, Albuquerque

Avoirdupois, No Doubt
Short and fat and dark, mostly, and some of them
speak French. Real nice.
Waitress, St. Louis, Missouri

Play *Oh Canada*, They'll All Stand Up
Canadians are so much like Americans we have no idea when
they're in town. I know Canadians don't like to hear that, they
like to think we are different, but I can't see it. After all, a lot of
the prominent people in this city at one time or another have
been Canadians, and they get along just fine.
Public relations director, New York City tourist bureau

More Than Mounties, I Guess
It's kind of a wild place, barren, with wide open spaces, not many people, Indians, that sort of thing. I still think of it as a place with Mounties, you know, from the movies, but I guess that isn't true so much now. I mean, you still have the Mounties, but you have other people, too.

Law student, American University, Washington, DC

Great Expectations
Mostly they're friendly, but sometimes they're pretty fussy. The least thing goes wrong and they're out saying, "We spent a lot of money to come down here, and we expect better than this." Tough titty.

Waiter, Key West, Florida

Brothers Under the Divorce Decree
They're exactly the same as Americans, except for the strange money. Exactly. I ought to know, I was married to one.

Waitress, Staples, Minnesota

Politics

A Kind Word for Parliament
You couldn't have a situation like what happened in Vietnam under the parliamentary system like what they have in Canada. Have you read General Westmorland's book? [*A Soldier Reports,* by General William Westmorland, US commander in Vietnam] It's all in there. What happened was the executive and the legislature in Washington, they had a gap between them. Boy, did they have a gap. The President was fighting the war, but the Congress was against it, and it got all screwed up, because you can't fight a war that way. Under the parliamentary system, the legislature has got to do what the leadership says, or kick out the guy and put in somebody else. They work together. I guess there are maybe disadvantages I don't know about, but that's one thing I really admire about Canada is the parliamentary system.
Retired colonel, US Air Force,
Upper Sandusky, New York

For One Thing, You Don't Buy Our Wheat
The communist countries can always get along and get together on things, why can't Canada and the United States?
Police officer, Philadelphia

Snarl Quietly, Please
I'm sometimes surprised and upset by the blatant anti-Americanism you get. People are very open about it. In Calais, there used to be bad feelings about Canada, but nobody would say anything to a Canadian. In Antigonish, they aren't a bit shy about telling me. What makes it a little silly is that I can't see any difference between Canadians and Americans.
University student from Calais, Maine,
attending St. Francis Xavier University

High On Canada

I'll tell you one thing about Canada, they don't just jump on your neck automatically. Almost everywhere you go or read about, somebody is giving Uncle Sam hell for something he did or didn't do, or might have done or should have done, or shouldn't have done and as far as most of the world is concerned, we can just go fart in a corner. Well, that kind of thing gets to you after a while, but when something comes up that involves the Canadians, you can talk about it in some sort of atmosphere of reasonableness. Even if we disagree like hell, even if we say this and they say that, and we aren't ever going to agree, you don't get this feeling of unremitting, blind, blanket hostility, and that's why I'm high on Canada. She's one of the few friends we've got we can count on no matter what.

US Information Administration official,
Washington, DC

Not To Mention The Taxes

Look around here, you want to see some Canadians. Doctors. You'll see a lot of Canadian doctors came down here to get away from that godawful socialized medicine they've got up there. That and the weather.

Physician, Phoenix, Arizona

Medicare And The Red Scare

A nation that is rapidly becoming a nation turning to state socialism, and I can give you chapter and verse. Point number one, they have state automobile insurance up there, where you have to have insurance and you have to buy it from the government. They can charge you what they like, and if you don't like it, to hell with you. The service is lousy and everything, they've got a hell of a mess on their hands; but that's what you get when you turn your back on the free enterprise system that everybody wants to knock these days. The kids, you hear the kids talking about politics, you'd think free enterprise was terrible. And what are the kids doing, sitting around on their asses is what, telling us how things should be, only they're too busy getting soused to do it themselves. So there's your number one point.

34

Number two is that they have a lot of socialist governments up there. I don't mean left wing, or Democratic, or anything like that, these birds call themselves socialists and run on the platform. They're proud of it. I forgot the name, it's something about Democratic, but it's not Democratic, it's socialist. A Jewish fella heads it up. They run in like the state elections, provinces, and they've got three or four of these birds elected as heads of the provinces. So there's another thing, you've got socialist governments up there.

Point number three is my business. I'm a doctor. Up in Canada, the doctors all work for the State. Literally. Just like Russia. Only, they're better paid, of course. At one of our conventions, we had a speaker, he was a Canadian, came from Canada, from Saskatchewan or one of those places out west. He told us what was going on as regards the medical profession in Canada, and it's going right the same way as what happened in England when the socialists got in control there. State medicine. And state medicine is bad medicine for the patient.

They've got hospitals up there, overcrowded, beds in the corridors, people lined up and all that. We have some crowding, I'm not saying we don't, but at least we're doing something about it here. Up there, they just don't care any more. They've given up, like Russia.

Doctors can't even prescribe what they give their patients. The doctor isn't the doctor any more, he's just another bureaucrat working for the State.

A lot of the doctors don't like it, and they're coming to their senses the way they did in England when they had that stuff. Young ones, especially, they're getting out. They had a doctors' strike up there, and the doctors were ordered back to work, and of course the doctors went because the doctor is a good citizen.

And point number four is – I forget point number four because I always get so goddamn mad about point number three. I don't care what some people say, I tell you Canada is headed for a hell of a mess. Did you get all that?

Physician, Cleveland, Ohio

Far Out And Far Right
I used to be all in favour of Canada. Some of my best friends, and all that bullshit. But that was up until they elected that commie

Prime Minister. Trudeau is his name. A commie, everybody knows it. A fellow from out west, he got up in the Congress and said it right out, that the Prime Minister of Canada was a commie. Well, I naturally expected that to be the end of Mr. Trudeau. No such thing. If they didn't go and put him right back in the next time. All I can say is, that was the end of Canada, as far as I'm concerned, and I don't care who knows it.

Farmer near Rutland, Vermont

Right Winged, Left-Handed?

I have the papers at home but I haven't filled them out yet for an immigrant visa. I'm tremendously attracted by the politics. Canada seems a more socialist kind of country that the US. It's not socialist, you could even call it right wing in some things, but you have things like socialized medicine up there, and the railway owned by the government, and the airline, and things like that. If it is right wing, it's a better kind of right wing than we have here. Canada didn't get into the Vietnam War, and to me that's terribly important, politically. And there's a greater acceptance that the government should step into the economy and straighten things out. Here you leave everything up to private enterprise, and just take your chances.

Librarian, Albuquerque, New Mexico

A New Era

There are political problems building up, no question about that . . .

There is an edge to the argument that you didn't used to hear. Hell, we can't even agree anymore on what we're arguing about. We had a merry-go-round a while back over the balance-of-trade figures. We said this country was running a substantial deficit in trade with Canada, and your people produced perfectly reputable figures that said, no, you were running a substantial deficit with us.

So we would go into negotiations, with your people saying "In view of the substantial deficit in our balance of trade, we think you should give way on this matter or that," and we would say, "In view of *our* substantial deficit in balance-of-trade, we think Canada should be more forthcoming."

Finally, the whole thing had to be put over to an international

36

committee, and they discovered, what everybody already knew, that we were measuring things in different ways. So they finally came up with some compromise figures that showed nobody running a substantial deficit anywhere. Not that it solved much, because our side said the solution was political, and the figures cooked, and now what are we going to do about this substantial deficit of trade? And your side said the same.

So this is a new era. There is no longer an assumption that Canada should get favours from us, or indeed that Canada needs favours from us. We think you're a little slow catching on. You want to be treated as a sovereign, independent nation except when being treated that way is going to hurt your trade.

Canada is a big boy in the international scene now, and we don't appreciate it when you act as if you were in the same spot you were in some years ago.

You could afford to be more liberal in your trade dealings. You could afford, for instance, to buy an American plane as a replacement for the Argus without a lot of anguish and soul-searching about giving business to the perfidious Yankees. [Note: We did.] You really ought to grow up.

Department of State official, Washington, DC

God Bless Back-sass

The Canadian penchant for masochism really comes out during Question Period in the House of Commons. . .[When I was stationed] in Ottawa, and there was something we weren't sure about, we would just wait until somebody asked the appropriate question in Parliament, and then file a report. . . It's a great system, I'm really all for it, because your government is always out there, under the gun. It's not the same here, when the President gives a press conference. He's not being questioned by people who consider themselves his equals, and there's no back-sass. When you saw David Lewis go after Trudeau, you really got fireworks. It seems to me it's harder to keep things concealed up there. Take when the Gray Report [on US investment in Canada] was floating around. We wanted, naturally, to know what was in that report as soon as possible. Well, out it came, as you remember. [It was leaked to *The Canadian Forum* magazine.] There was no way to keep it back. I admire that openness in the Canadian system, even if some Canadian government officials don't.

State Department official, Washington, DC

In a Nutshell, Tu As Raison
A lot of the people speak French and a lot of the other people
don't. And those that don't don't like those that do. I read that in
the paper.
Security guard, Banning, California

Why Not? He's Looking for Work
The President is elected by Parliament, not by the
people. That makes it easier to get rid of him. You
would never get a Nixon in Canada. The Parliament
wouldn't let him.
Student, University of Tennessee, Nashville

Point No Fingers
They've got a funny system up there, politics-wise. They don't
have a president or any of that, and you can have an election any
time and they still have a royal family. It looks funny to us, but
with what we've got right now, who the hell are we to point the
finger?
Insurance salesman, Chicago

Aw, What's A Revolution Between Friends?
I think Canada's just like here, except you didn't have
a revolution.
*Architecture student, University of New
Mexico, Albuquerque*

We Don't Hate Each Other
Bumming around Europe, you used to come across Canadians
and they always seemed very attractive to me. They were more
open than Americans, more relaxed. Maybe they were more at
home, because a number of them spoke French. The funny
thing was, they didn't talk about politics the way we do, there
wasn't the same virulent strain in their comments. I guess that
says something about Canadian politics. They don't hate each
other the way we do.
Graduate student, Harvard Business School

That's Okay, Neither Do We
I have never understood the French-English bilingual problem in Canada. I understand the problem, but I don't understand the basis of it. One group speaks English and the other speaks French, so big deal. We hear about strikes and protests, but our media coverage of Canada is so rotten I don't even know what the hell it's all about.
Engineer, Denver, Colorado

Gad!
When things go wrong in Canada, when there's racism or violence or miscarriage of justice, they just hush it up. Stiff upper lip and all that. They're just the same as the British that way.
Radio reporter, Pittsburgh

Chipping In And Butting Out
The Canadian labour movement is going through a very nationalist phase right now, and I don't know how long it's going to last. Maybe a very long time. There's two sides to it, of course. A lot of us feel that if it weren't for the international unions – the steelworkers, autoworkers, yeah, and the paperworkers, too, the Canadian labour movement wouldn't have gotten very far. So we kind of resent it when we're told to butt out, as is happening more and more often. On the other side, a union leader has got to represent his guys and I wouldn't have much respect for one who didn't. At the last AFL-CIO convention, there was quite a lot of fuss about this. Our guys were saying, "Look we have to protect Canadian jobs, too, they're our guys," and other guys were pushing the Burke-Hartke bill [a restrictive trade bill that would limit imports of manufactured goods to the US]. We were caught in a bind. The Burke-Hartke thing wasn't aimed at Canada, but just the same, if you're going to protect American jobs, that means you're going to hurt Canadian jobs. In our industry, there's no other way. So the old solidarity went right out the window and we had the Canadians screaming about getting the dirty end of the stick. I'd have said the same thing in their shoes. So the way I see it, as long as the economic going is rough, you're going to get this nationalist feeling on both sides of the border and it could become kind of permanent, which might or might not be a good thing for Canada in the long run.
Paperworkers' Union official, Washington, DC

Girls
and Boys
Together

Maybe He Was Just Playing Doctor
My daughter lived with a Canadian doctor in San Francisco. He
seemed real nice, he was very generous and kind, kind of a tubby
fella, but friendly. He didn't marry her, though.
Saleslady, Minot, North Dakota

No Comment
**Canadian broads are really something. Big tits, big
asses, yeah, husky dames. They're all right, you treat
them right.**
Autoworker, Detroit

A Touch of Class
Canadian women have a certain cachet, I don't know exactly
how to put this, but a certain culture, not at all the backwoods
primitive you see in the movie version. Canadian women dress
beautifully, walk beautifully, sophisticated. I suspect it's the
French strain. The French, you know, are very sophisticated,
too.
Traveller in dental supplies, Louisville, Kentucky

You Mean Beavers, Surely
Canadian girls screw like minks, man. If you don't
believe me, go down to Fort Lauderdale and check for
yourself. Man, they just don't care.
Bookstore Clerk, New York City

Power of the Moustache
The boys are real cute, you know. Moustaches and that, sexy, you
know. We went down to Florida one time, and there was this
bunch of boys from Canada down for holidays, came down to
have a little fun. And, well . . . I'm not going to go on with this.
Waitress, Buffalo, New York

Welcoming
Canadian girls are very welcoming. We met these two girls at
Daytona Beach, and there was none of this futzing around you
get with American girls. That was the goddamnedest weekend
I ever spent in my life. They were from Quebec or something.
Veterinary student, Bethesda, Maryland

Hanging Loose
I find Canadian men tremendously attractive. They're
much more open than Americans, not so uptight, and
not so selfish.
Law student, Harvard, Boston

It's Enough
The boys are cute, that's all I know about Canada.
High School student, Fremont, Ohio

The Lost Decade
The Canadian male is a chauvinist pig, about ten years
behind here.
TV production assistant, New York City

Dialogue On L Street In Washington

"Hey, honey! Hey, you wanna go out with me?"

"No, thank you, but I'm glad you stopped me. I'd like to ask you a question."

"What kinna question?"

"I'm from Canada. Do you have many Canadian clients? Do you know anything about Canada?"

"You puttin' me on?"

"No, no . . ."

"You a cop or somethin'?"

"No, just a journalist, relentlessly pursuing the facts."

"Huh?"

"Do you know anything about Canadians?"

"No, honey, I don't but if they all like you, they a poor bunch of peckers."

"I'll put you down as 'Undecided.' "

A Scientific Sampling . . .

Canadians are nice and polite, not rude and noisy like some of the Americans you see. They're just friendly people and kinda cute. 'Course I've only met but two Canadians I know of; they sure were cute.

Hotel desk clerk, Port Jervis, New York

Sure, Europeanality — Means Dumb

I'm terribly impressed with the – I don't want to use the word stupidity – with the Europeanality of Canadian women. We spend our summers in Muskoka, in Ontario, and I have the most dreadful time making conversation with the women from Toronto who are up there. I think Canada is beautiful and I love living there, the people are great to me but this one thing is just appalling, and they do it to their children, too. This docility, submission to the male; we have it here with our immigrant women when they first come in, but as soon as they've been here awhile they get over it and begin to speak up. Not the Canadian women. You ask them when they've read lately and they say, "Oh, I've been too busy looking after the children." They don't want to talk about politics or any-thing, they just follow whatever the husband says.

Minister's wife, Grand Rapids, Michigan

Ah, Memory

We went up to Quebec one time, our high school class, it was like a class project, for history it was. The Seven Years War and all that, and the seige of Quebec when Benedict Arnold and that other fellow went up there and they all died in the snow – not Arnold – and they never did take the place. Well, anyway, we stayed at this big old hotel, Chateau something, and it was just the nicest place, all the narrow streets and old buildings and monuments. They got a monument to a farmer out in front of City Hall, I never forgot that. I never saw a monument to a farmer before. It made you feel kind of solemn, you know? But what I really remember are the boys. They would be kind of hanging around in the park near the hotel or down along there was a kind of boardwalk thing there, down along that. And when we'd come out, they'd come up, with their accent and all, and say could they help us. "Mademoiselle," they called us, "Mademoiselle, are you having a good time?" they'd say. Well, of course, our teacher beat them off like a stick, almost. They were the best-looking boys. "Mademoiselle, are you having a good time?" I'll never forget that, and God knows, it wasn't yesterday.

Housewife, Columbus, Ohio

Well, There's the Pill

We were there for EXPO '67, the World's Fair, in 1967, and all I can remember is the big crowds, and a ride that scared the hell out of me, and the girls. There are more pretty girls per acre in Canada than any place I ever seen. It's a wonder the population isn't double what it is.

Carpenter, Toledo, Ohio

Northern Southerners?

The men are polite, more polite than here. If you get on an elevator and a man takes off his hat, chances are he's either a Canadian or a Southerner, they're the only polite ones left. I suppose that sounds old-fashioned these days, but I like polite men, and I like Canada.

Flower store clerk, Washington, DC

Our Cities

Toronto
I just love Canada, I think it's the sweetest place in the whole, wide world. If I had to live anywhere but North Carolina, it'd be in Canada. 'Course, I don't know anything but Toronto, but it's just the nicest place. It's so clean, not like an American city. And you can go out walking, even at night. One night, I had hay fever and my eyes were like to burning out of my head. I got up – this was 5 a.m. in the morning – and went for a walk right down University Avenue. Five a.m., and you didn't get raped or anything. You sure couldn't do that here.
Secretary, Charlotte, North Carolina

I understand they are changing up there, up around Toronto. It's taken over as the dominant city in Canada, and they're becoming more industrialized, faster paced, just like the United States.
Architecture student, University of New Mexico, Albuquerque

We lived in Toronto for a year and a half, this was about ten years ago. It was just starting to come to life. When we first went, you couldn't go to a movie on Sunday, or anything. Later, it became quite exciting, and from what I hear now, it's about the nicest city in North America.
Advertising executive, Washington, DC

44

I only been there once. Last year. Toronto. It's the shits.
Community college student, Washington, DC

Here is a city, Toronto, that has taken charge of its own destiny, laid down rules for development, said to the world, "Well, this is going to be a city, with a downtown where people can live and breathe and walk, not a beehive by day and a jungle by night." Very impressive.
Researcher, National Rifle Association, Washington, DC

Well, the one thing I remember about visiting Toronto is that you can read the map on the subway. In New York, I just get lost, I spend hours wandering around all over the place, and I never know where I'll end up. But Toronto's such a neat, itty-bitty little place, you can't get lost.
Housewife, Purvis, North Carolina

I went up there last year to visit some friends playing in a band. You ever hear of the Mutch Brothers? They weren't very popular but they played for Peter Stuyvesant cigarettes. We were in Toronto and Mississauga and that other place, what's its name? Ottawa. Real nice. Toronto's got an island, we went there. You go by ferry from downtown and there's this island park right there. Real nice.
Gas station attendant, Louisville, Kentucky

Toronto's a terrific place, the police go around in little yellow Volkswagens. *Zoom, zoom,* up and down the streets. You haven't seen anything till you've seen a cop in a yellow bug.
Secretary, Blacksburg, South Carolina

Montreal

I was in Montreal and found it very exciting, a big city that hadn't gone wrong. Very friendly and open. International, with two languages. I don't think of Canada as a backwoods place because of Montreal, I guess Toronto wouldn't be as international, but it's up to date.

Housewife, Portland, Maine

For Americans, Stupid

I went to Montreal for a week in the middle of the winter and I was never cold once. I stayed at the Bonaventure, and you can go everywhere underground; movies, restaurants, stores, it's all there and you don't have to go outside. If the Canadians are so fond of winter, why did they build it like that?

Salesman, Cincinnati, Ohio

I was up in Montreal last spring. I like it, it was beautiful, but what disturbed me was the attitude, a posh, upper-class chic city very conscious of being chic. A real self-conscious city. Toronto is not so self-conscious, but it's a very fast-growing city. Whether that's good will remain to be seen.

Graduate student, Harvard University

Of course, Montreal is the same as any big city and I got in Toronto, in particular, a sense of tremendous growth. Dallas north. You might as well be in any comparable American city.

Lawyer, Cambridge, Massachusetts

I saw a special on television all about Canada preparing for the Olympics and they had the Montreal mayor on there. He was incredible, the way he could commit the whole country to spend a billion dollars on a mess like that and nobody dares to say boo to him. You wouldn't have an American mayor getting away with a thing like that, not even Richard Daley.

Housewife, Chicago, Illinois

Quebec
They speak French up in Canada, not all over the place, just in Quebec. It's a real nice city, though, Quebec City, so old and beautiful. I went there with my boss, and he kept walking around and shouting, "Lead me to somebody who speaks English," and everybody laughed.
State civil servant, Raleigh, North Carolina

Victoria vs Vancouver
The wife and I went up to Canada one time and it was real nice. We took the ferry from Port Angelus and went to Victoria. It was a real pretty city, all the people were real friendly. Just a nice place, not like Vancouver. We went to Vancouver and stayed in a big motel. At night they locked all the doors and couldn't nobody get in. I asked them why and she said it was because there was so much vandalism and all. Vancouver is a big city, like some place in California, lots of traffic, lot of hustle and nobody seems to have any time for you, time to say hello or anything. We didn't like it. Canadians other places were friendly, though.
Tire dealer, Grangeville, Idaho

I've been to Vancouver and Victoria. It's a really beautiful city, Victoria. Vancouver's just a city.
Businessman, Sacramento, California

Far Out
Canada – just to say the name gives me goosebumps. It's so romantic. Vancouver, Canada or Montreal, Canada – when I see that in the paper it's like reading Paris, France. It has a faraway, exciting ring to it.
Typist, Albuquerque, New Mexico

The
Territorial
Imperative:
1838-93

The extraordinary closeness of Canadian-American relations in the mid-twentieth century has tended to dazzle our after-dinner speakers into forgetting how much of our history has been marked by outright hostility between the two nations, and naked lust, on the part of the Americans, for our fair, white body. This section begins with President Mark Van Buren's lament about the role Americans played in the Rebellion in Upper Canada, but soon settles down to the theme of the period from the 1830s to the turn of the century. A good many Americans thought Canada belonged by right to them, and a lamentable number of Canadians agreed.

December, 1838: A Regrettable Invasion
I had hoped that the respect for the laws and regard for the peace and honour of their own country, which has ever characterized the citizens of the United States, would have prevented any portion of them from using any means to promote insurrection in the territory of a power with which we are at peace, and with whom the United States are desirous of maintaining the most friendly relations. I regret, deeply, however, to be obliged to inform you that this has not been the case.

Information has been given to me, derived from official and other sources, that many citizens of the United States have associated together to make hostile incursions from our territory into Canada and to aid and abet insurrection there, in violation of the obligations and laws of the United States and in open disregard of their own duties as citizens. This information has been in part confirmed, by a hostile invasion actually made by citizens of the United States, in conjunction with Canadians and others, and accompanied by a forcible seizure of the property of our citizenry, and an application thereof to the prosecution of military authority against the authorities and people of Canada. The results of these criminal assaults upon the peace and order of a neighbouring country have been, as was to be expected, fatally destructive to the misguided or deluded persons engaged in them, and highly injurious to those on whose behalf they are professed to have been undertaken.

President Mark Van Buren, Message to Congress, describing an abortive raid made by Americans in support of William Lyon Mackenzie

1842: Not Only That, It Hurts

Great Britain, in hanging, shooting or transporting American citizens who were assisting the Canadian revolution has infringed upon the rights of free men.

Resolution passed by the city of Buffalo, NY

1844: The Line Is Drawn

Fifty-four Forty, or Fight!

Senator William Allen, in debate on the Oregon Boundary dispute. Allen, and many other Americans, wanted the Oregon-Canada boundary drawn at 54°40' North, which would have given the US all of British Columbia's coast up to Prince Rupert. Presidential nominee James K. Polk agreed, but after he became president, Britain and the US settled on the 49th parallel, and didn't fight.

July, 1845: Manifest Destiny

[It is] our Manifest Destiny to overspread the continent alloted by Providence for the free development of our multiplying millions.

The July-August issue of United States Magazine and Democratic Review

1849: Another Invitation to be Liberated

Be It Resolved that, in the true spirit of Democracy, deeply sympathizing with the downtrodden, oppressed and over-restricted of every clime and country, we hail with joy the rising spirit of liberty in the Provinces of Canada as expressed recently in the published opinions of its citizens on the subject of annexation; that we appreciate the efforts and emulate the movements of the friends of Republicanism in Canada, and that we cordially extend to them the hand of friendship, fellowship and brotherly love; that we will use all peaceable means in our power to further their object in becoming members of this our glorious union of free and independent and sovereign states.

Resolution passed by the Democratic state convention, Montpelier, Vermont

1851: Travel Note
Farewell, old master,
Don't come after me,
I'm on my way to Canada
Where coloured men are free.
Anonymous slave song

January 10, 1853: Worth Looking At

There is a country and there is a people competent for self-government, that are prepared to take upon themselves the responsibilities of free men, and which we may find in our interest to receive among us – I mean peaceably – and allow them to become a part and parcel of this country, and I care not how soon. I refer, Mr. Chairman, to the whole British possessions upon the north, containing an area of two millions, two hundred and fifty-two thousand, three hundred and ninety-five square miles. That is something worth looking at . . .The annexation of that territory to this Union (to use terms of gentlemen) Destiny has ordained, and it will ere long take place.

> *Representative Bell of Ohio, in debate. Bell spoke at a time when relations between the countries were so cordial that an act for Reciprocal Trade (i.e., no tariff barriers on either side) was passed in the US a year later. However, with the onset of the US Civil War, and Britain's obvious sympathy with the Confederacy (Britain controlled Canada's foreign policy), relations soon soured, and Reciprocity died a-borning.*

December 31, 1861: Snivelling Cant from Suckling Britons

Out of this Trent affair has come one permanent good. The old, natural, instinctive, and wise distrust and dislike for England is revived again in the American heart, and will outlive all the soft words and snivelling cant about international brotherhood and reciprocity. These are "our Canadian brethren," these suckling Britons to whom, like fools, we have opened our ports. . .These reciprocal brethren of ours have been ready to fly at our throats from the moment when they felt it safe to be insolent.

Editorial in the Buffalo Express, *inspired by the fact that when the British mail packet* Trent *was stopped and inspected by a Union warship, two Confederate spies were discovered aboard, skulking. The Trent Affair brought all manner of editorial writers out of their lairs, breathing fire. The* Chicago Tribune *suggested that:*

The North. . .should take Canada by the throat. . .and throttle her as a St. Bernard would throttle a poodle pup.

December, 1864: Aftermath of the St. Alban's Raid

Confederate raiders, operating out of Canadian sanctuaries, crossed the border in a series of lightning raids on the northern US, the most serious of which was on the village of St. Alban's, Vermont. Not surprisingly, northern Americans were apoplectic, and the New York Herald Tribune *warned:*

The next raid is likely to be venged upon the nearest Canadian village which gives refuge to the marauders.

Abraham Lincoln expressly forbade Union troops from crossing the border in "hot pursuit," but General Joseph Hanson wrote that:

In case a raid should be attempted from Canada I intend that somebody shall be hurt if I have to go into Canada to do it. Then if exception is taken, that can be adjusted by negotiation afterward.

There was even a campaign song, with the chorus:

And we'll go and capture Canada,
For we've nothing else to do.

And an annexationist version of "Yankee Doodle" that went:

Secession first he would put down
Wholly and forever,
And afterwards from Britain's crown
He Canada would sever.

July, 1865: Annexation Again

After the war, talk of annexation sprang up again, and for about thirty years, with some exceptions, American comment about Canada tended towards the possessive.

I believe that in two years from the abrogation of the Reciprocity Treaty the People of Canada themselves will apply for admission to the United States.

John Potter, American consul in Montreal

June 27, 1867: And It's Not Nice To Fool Mother Nature

I know that Nature designs that this whole continent, not merely these thirty-six states, shall be, sooner or later, within the magic circle of the American Union.

William Seward, US Secretary of State

March, 1868: With Two Boxtops, Of Course

The cession of Northern British America to the United States, accompanied by the construction of a Northern Pacific Railroad should be regarded by Great Britain and Canada as satisfactory provisions of a treaty which shall remove all grounds of controversy between the respective countries.

Resolution passed by the Minnesota state legislature

April, 1869: Come Along Quietly

There is no one in this country who desires the annexation of one of their provinces unless the mass of the population desire it. Should they, in obedience to a natural law of centripedal force, gravitate to us, we will welcome them cordially.

Editorial in the Portland, Oregon, Press

July 31, 1869: A Dissenting Voice

We do not know as we want Canada very bad. We had better become Reconstructionists, secure our finances, and see if we are able to take good care of what we have before assuming charge of much more.

Editorial in the St. Paul, Minnesota, Daily Pioneer

September, 1869: I Say, Not Victoria, Old Chap
The Fenians of the Pacific and a few thousand willing Americans and Germans will take away all that country from the British. We will lower their flag in six months . . . We will give our notes at ninety days for [an invasion force] and be back with the spoils of Victoria to pay them before they are due.

> *Editorial in the Portland, Oregon,* Herald. *The Fenians were Irish sympathizers who hoped to get back at Britain by attacking Canada. They did, in fact, mount a number of raids – on Campobello Island, Fort Erie, and the Eastern Townships. They did not, however, take Victoria.*

November 24, 1869: Take Me Back To The Star-Spangled Valley . . .
If the Revolutionists of the Red River are encouraged and sustained by the avowed sympathy of the American people, we may . . . see the Stars and Stripes wave from Fort Garry, from the waters of Puget Sound, along the shores of Vancouver.

> *Ignatius Donnelly, speaking at St. Paul, Minnesota. Donnelly was an adventurer who hoped to take advantage of the first Riel Rebellion – as we had taken advantage of the Civil War, and Americans of the 1837 Rebellions – to raise a little free-lance hell.*

April 22, 1870: The Continental Creed
This continent is ours and we may as well notify the world that we will fight for our own if we must.

> **Senator Zachariah Chandler, in debate**

1870: Destiny Rides Again
That it is the Destiny of the United States to possess the whole of the northern continent I fully believe . . . Our destiny, which must not, cannot, be altered – a fiat which has the potency of irrevocable law – the forward march of Americanization until the whole continent shall be but one nation, with one sovereign government, one flag, one people.

> *Elwood Evans, in a political speech*

January 9, 1881: A Cooling Word
We have really nothing to gain from [annexation] in a
social and intellectual point of view, and next to
nothing in a commercial way.
Editorial in the New York Sun

June, 1881: Menuabilia
The annex of the New York Public Library contains a
vintage collection of Canadiana, including the menu of a
dinner meeting of the American Society of Civil Engineers,
held in Montreal in July, 1881. On the menu are scribbled
two notes that caught my eye, obviously written for a
Canadian friend by Americans. One reads:
We will hold fast to good impressions, and let the evil be
remembered only to help us avoid them [sic] in the future.
Charles Latimer, Cleveland, Ohio

It must have been quite a dinner. It also sent another
engineer into a paroxysm of near-poetry:
No line 'twixt the United States and Canada. It has been
obliterated by the Institute of Civil Engineers and their lady
associates.
Signature undecipherable

1887: The Seals Get Into The Act
It is proposed by the colony of a foreign nation [i.e., Canada] in
defiance of the joint remonstrance of all the countries interested,
to destroy this business [the sealing trade] by the indiscriminate
slaughter and extermination of the animals in question, in the
open neighbouring sea, during the period of gestation, when the
common dictates of humanity ought to protect them, were no
interest at all involved. And it is suggested that we are prevented
from defending ourselves against such depradations because the
sea at a certain distance from the coast is free. The same line of
argument would take under its protection piracy and the slave
trade, when prosecuted in the open sea.
Edward John Phelps, US ambassador to Britain, complaining bitterly
(and rightly) about the conduct of our seal fisheries

GOODS PROHIBITED, BUT *EVILS* ADMITTED.

MISS CANADA.—"NOW, MR. PREMIER, I DON'T PROPOSE TO ALLOW THIS COUNTRY TO BE MADE A SLAUGHTER-MARKET FOR AMERICAN IDEAS, ANY MORE THAN FOR AMERICAN GOODS."

from A Caricature History
of Canadian Politics,
published by Peter Martin
Associates Limited

1889: But Not Rotten To The Core, I Hope

Canada is like an apple on a tree just beyond reach. We may strive to grasp it, but the bough recedes from our hold just in proportion to our effort to catch it. Let it alone, and in due time it will fall into our hands.

James G. Blaine, Secretary of State

September 23, 1891: No Intercourse Makes A Hard Row

The fact is, we do not want any intercourse with Canada except through the medium of a tariff, and she will find she has a hard row to hoe and will ultimately, I believe, seek admission to the union.

James G. Blaine, in a letter to President Benjamin Harrison

November 6, 1893: Pax Americana

Union with Canada . . . will deliver the continent from any possible complications and add enormously to the power, influence, and prestige of North America. It would securely dedicate the continent to peaceful industry and progress.

Circular letter from the Continental Union League,
published in New York

Peaceable Us

We Call It "Paix"
When I think of Canada, I think ice, snow, real pretty
and white and clean. Peaceful, French and real nice.
An aide to the lieutenant governor of Alabama,
Point Clear, Alabama

Some Think It's Pink
I just think of Canada as that great orange expanse north of us.
Marine biology student, University of Hawaii

How About Red And White?
I think of blue, the colour blue, blue skies, blue water,
even royal blue.
Farm wife, LaFayette, Indiana, area

We Don't Have Ghettos – They're Called "Slums"
Canadians are polite and courteous and willing to take time with
people . . . And they aren't as violent as Americans. I grew up
with crime and I didn't realize how scary it was until I got out of
the ghetto and got away from it. Canadians don't have to go
through that.
Musician, Washington, DC

Mom Was Right

I've always admired Canada, because my mother visited there once, and she said it was nice and peaceful. I met some Canadian girls at school, and they were awful nice.

Receptionist, union headquarters,
Washington, DC

That Wasn't a Bomb, That Was a "Nuclear Device"

Canada has always stood for peace in my mind until they went and gave India the bomb. That was a very crappy thing to do and I couldn't understand it. Canada took a very major role as peacemaker in the Middle East and that in the Suez thing and here they are giving away the bomb to the Indians. Screwy thing to do. I can only assume that something's going on up there that we don't know about down here that would make them swing around like that.

Psychology major, Harvard

How About a Quiet Gangland Slaying?

They're supposed to be such a peaceable people but every time you pick up the paper it's a gangland slaying in Montreal or torch death of three or something. That doesn't sound too peaceable to me.

Political science major, University of Rochester, NY

Word From An Expert

I've always admired Canadians, they aren't violent, like Americans. That's nice.

Arms salesman from Tacoma, Washington, recently returned from a trip to South Korea, selling torpedo boats

Ouch!

You're the ones that gave India the bomb, aren't you?

Teaching assistant, University of Hawaii, Honolulu

Peacemaker

Canada will always be remembered by my generation as the nation that stood for peace, the nation other nations would trust to keep the peace, whether in the Middle East or Vietnam or Cyprus. If I were a Canadian, I would rather have that said about me than anything else.

Desk officer, Department of State, Washington, DC

Our Resources – and Theirs

Selling Water

Canadians are hyper on the subject, they think we're always after their resources. The fact is that if they want to sell us their water, it would be good for both of us. We could use the water, and for them, it means selling something that is just going to waste, now; it could be the most important crop they have, and constantly renewed.

Businessman, Salt Lake City, Utah

Fall Guys

Canada has a rapidly-growing labour force, and the policy of your government is to employ as much as possible of that labour force in manufacturing. You no longer want to be hewers of wood and drawers of water. Given Canada's geography and size, it's obvious that if most of your labour force is engaged in manufacturing, you are not going to be able to buy everything you make at home. That means exports, you've got to have all kinds of exports. So, there has been a substantial improvement in Canada's position, if you look at your exports from 1965 to the present, you will see that your net exports are up considerably.

I think this will continue; it is part of your public policy and it is a matter of necessity.

At the same time, we need Canadian resources, and, at a price, Canada is willing to sell those resources, be it wood pulp or iron ore or what have you.

At the same time, Canada needs a considerable influx of money to develop resources, particularly oil and gas.

When you put these three factors together – a growing manufacturing base, salable resources, and the need for capital – you can see a pattern emerging in which Canada will be pressing to keep a favourable balance of trade with the United States as a permanent part of your economy. Otherwise, the only way you can pay for the development of your resources is to run further and further into debt on an international basis.

So this has made Canada very aggressive in trade matters over the past few years. I see that trend continuing, but I also see an increasing resistance on this side of the border to being the fall guys. We understand what you're trying to do, but we have problems of our own, and we don't see why we should give you trade concessions so you can straighten out your books at the expense of ours.

So I foresee a period of tough, tough bargaining between our two countries, and I see it going on for quite a long period of time.

Department of Commerce official, Washington, DC

Pretty Poor

I'll tell you what burns me; this nation is running short of water and damn near out of natural gas, too. They got all kinds of water up north, just pouring out all over the place, but we can't have none. You drive out of town a ways, you'll see farms empty and houses deserted 'cause they bought them up, the city did, to get the water the farms use. That's how bad it is. You'll see industries closing down for lack of natural gas, and you'll see people up north, and that includes the Canadians, as far as I'm concerned, sitting on their asses and saying "No sir, you can't have any of that, it's ours." I call that pretty poor.

Farmer, near Red Rock, Arizona

Word For Our Side

Americans have become acutely aware of the problems of running short of crucial resources. If Canadians refuse to sell us their gas or water or any other resource because they fear they are going to need these things for the future, we understand that perfectly well, and we would do the same thing ourselves.

Professor of astronomy and solar heating expert, University of Arizona, Tucson

ALASKAN
99
OIL

CANADA

U.S.

The Old Double Cross
They're a bunch of double-crossers. The Minister of Energy was down here last year to assure us that while there would be oil cutbacks, they wouldn't hit us until about 1980. Then that guy [Donald Macdonald] was shuffled out of there and a new guy [Alastair Gillespie] was shuffled in and the first thing he was down here to say "Hold on, boys, we're going to start cutting you off in 1976, and it's going to get worse." Well, there's only one word for that, it's the old double cross.
Official in the Federal Energy Administration, Washington, DC

Kind of Sad
Attitudes towards Canada are undergoing a considerable shift. There was an editorial in this morning's paper [The Boston *Globe,* October 6, 1975] about the Alaska pipeline hassle in Washington. The editorial writer's point was that we should keep the movement entirely in American hands. He said sending the gas through Canada would be putting a major American resource in the hands of a foreign power. Like the Panama Canal situation. When I read that, I was profoundly shocked. I've never thought of Canada as a foreign power and I remember clearly that when the earlier continental pipeline was built, it went from your west, through the US and back up into Canada and nobody gave it a second thought. But that was in the 1950s, when that was set up. Now we're in the 1970s and things have changed. Americans can no longer assume that what is good for them suits Canada and vice versa. You have your own priorities and we have ours. So I wound up agreeing with that editorial writer, that we should keep our energy resources, including the transportation, under our own lock and key, and not assume that Canada will do whatever we want. In a way, I suppose that's a compliment to Canada, it shows you have achieved a certain level of independence and maturity up there. In another way, it's kind of sad.
Research scientist, Cambridge, Massachusetts

Fed Up
The Canadians are playing a double game with us, and I think it's going to backfire. They kept pushing the Mackenzie Valley Pipeline at us for bringing the gas in from the north, and when we said what guarantee can you give us that the provinces won't step in with some kind of tax and make it impossible to move gas from

66

Alaska through that line, they said, "Gee, we don't know, we'll have to think about that."

They were pretty rough in their opposition to the tankers down the west coast, but they have no real alternative to offer. They appear to be pretty rough on the El Paso deal, but what would they do instead? Frankly, we're fed up.

Energy Research and Development Agency official,
Germantown, Maryland

Too Damn Soft

How come they put up the oil, for Christ's sake? We did enough for Canada, two world wars and Vietnam and then they join the Arabs. Ask me, we're too damn soft on them, we don't have to take that crap from any place like Canada.

Gas station attendant, Homestead, Florida

The Co-Operative Spirit

I can understand that they don't want to give away their resources, that they might want to consider very carefully what to do with them. I can understand, too, the feeling that US investment might take over Canada, that is a very real fear. But really, our futures are bound together more than any other countries in the world, more than the US and Mexico, even. On these things, we are more or less homogeneous. I was on the board of directors of Michigan Gas, and we dealt with the gas that was coming from the Canadian West across the US and into the Canadian East. We had no trouble with allocations because it was done in an open, co-operative spirit, and that will always be the best for both of us.

Businessman, politician, and ex-mayor
of Grand Rapids, Michigan

Provincialism

If Canada had said okay to the Mackenzie Valley deal when it first came up, instead of humming and hawing and fooling around, gas would be moving down there now, and we would all be a hell of a lot better off. I just don't understand the narrow provincialism of the Canadians on resource policy.

Real estate dealer, Fairbanks, Alaska

Astronaut Eye-View

I think the period of looking at individual resources as belonging to a single nation is probably coming to a close. When you look at the world through the eyes of astronauts, it's hard to believe it can contain separate boundaries for these things. The world is a closed eco-system with shared resources and shared unhappiness. We are just beginning to understand now that when people are in trouble on the other side of the world, we are all in trouble. We are just beginning to understand that there is a finite limit to growth, with all that entails in the terms of the use of resources. In such a world, can one nation stand aside? I think not. There is a reluctance, perhaps, to commit Canadian resources to the care and control of the United States – the fear that this nation hasn't done too well with our own resources. The trouble is that our technological capabilities still exceed our social capabilities. In the field of technology, we can do just about anything we set our minds to do, the question is no longer "Can we do it?", but "Should we do it?" We are going to have to put a lot more effort into answering that question than we have in the past, but the need is now being recognized in the United States Congress. So I come back to where I began and say that, given the proper use of these resources, I think it necessary and inevitable that Canada's hoard be shared, not with the US, but with the world.

Vice president of a resource development company,
Cambridge, Massachusetts

All There

Canada is absolutely vital to this country. There is no nation in the world that can compare with Canada as a safe, reliable supply of needed resources. Political stability is there, the resources are there, the friendship is there, and the need for American dollars is there. It's all there.

Research assistant, oil company, New York City

Just Take It

I think if we need it and they won't give it to us, we should just take it.

National guardsman, Fremont, Ohio

Cautionary Note

If the Canadians turn over their resources to us after the way the big corporations have screwed around the resources of this country, well, they're just crazy, is all I can say.

Student, University of Arizona, Tucson

We Need Each Other

There is a great community of need, if not of spirit, I have always felt. We both face the same problems in energy, although it is more acute here. Canada will have the problem, too, you wait and see. Perhaps that is not seen yet in Canada, but it will be. You have great pools of resources in one country but not the capital or expertise to get it out. We have the capital and the expertise, but we are running short of oil at a reasonable price. In a situation like that, what could be more natural than that we should get closer together? That is why I always resent it when some politician steps in and interferes and makes trouble between the two countries. We need each other too much, energy-wise, to get into stupid disputes.

Gas company official, Dallas, Texas

Uncle Sam On Guard

You're not just talking about oil, about how much it's gonna cost to drive your car down to the supermarket, for Christ's sake, you're talking about defence, about freedom. I was in the navy, worked on oil supplies, saw the whole thing. If you can't control supplies, you can't fight a war, can't win it, anyway. You can be cut off. You have to have things under your own control. You can't depend on these Arab countries, that's bullshit. They're too unstable, first thing you know, boom, up goes everything. You've got to have your supplies here, in North America. That means uranium, nuclear plants, all that stuff, but most important for now it means you've got to have oil, oil and gas, under some kind of sensible continental control. Canadians go ape when they hear this, but it's time they grew up and realized the facts. If Canada wants to sit on its oil and gas, I guess that's okay, I guess it's up to you, but if you do, there won't be any oil and gas to fuel the fleets and armies that have to defend you. The Russians or Chinese or anybody can come walking in over the Pole and there's not one damn thing you can do about it. And old Uncle Sam won't be able to do anything, either, because he's going to be too busy trying to get his own oil and gas for himself.

Canadians always think the argument for continental resource development is because the big oil companies want to get rich. That's bullshit. Of course we want to get rich, who doesn't? But we're talking about more than money here, we're talking about the kind of world you want to live in, and your kids, too.

Canada can get up on her high horse and say no oil for the goddamn Yankees, but that would be a serious mistake. And if I had my way, we wouldn't just stand around and watch it happen. I think I've said more than enough.

Executive, New York-based international
resource company

Okay Proceed John-wise?

Our company has always done a considerable amount of business in Canada, and in recent years we have tried to make sure Canadian-born people were in charge of our Canadian operation. There was quite a bit of fuss about this sort of thing up there, and you could see their point, to a degree. Frankly, it hasn't worked out too well. I have always had to treat my Canadian managers very lightly indeed. They're a tetchy bunch. But what's worse, they tend to dwell on insignificant things, and to dawdle away their time. Christ, I wouldn't be surprised if I got a Telex asking for permission to go to the toilet.

Energy company executive, Dallas, Texas

The Great
(and Not So Great)
Outdoors

No Prize, But Our Heartiest Congratulations
Canada, that's up north, near New York State, isn't it? Only it's
not a state, it's a whole country. Is that right? Do I win a prize?
  Liquor store clerk, Albuquerque

Of Course, That's Why We Have an Open-Door Policy
I think of Canada as an outdoor country and of the United
States as an indoor country. I think of the important things
that happen happening outside up there, and inside down
here, and that is a very important difference. Maybe it's stupid,
but that's what I think.
  University of Virginia student, Charlottesville

Trouble In The North
I've never been to Canada but the one time. My wife's cousin
used to do a lot of fishing up there, he said it was the greatest
fishing in the world. It seemed like a tolerable long way to go,
all the way from Alabama, but one time I agreed I'd go along,
just to see. We went to a fishing lodge out of Kenora, Ontario,
and it was the damnedest place I ever did see, a great big, huge
place, a wooden mansion more like than any fishing lodge I
ever saw. Well sir, the first thing that happened was that they
told us we couldn't eat the fish. You could catch them, but you

71

couldn't eat them . . . They were full of mercury. Yes, sir, right up there in the middle of the wilderness, full of mercury . . .

Well, we got us a guide, an Indian, maybe forty, maybe fifty years old. It was hard to tell. I would say he looked sixty, but he had his son along and the boy couldn't have been more than ten, so I figure he was younger than sixty. We had a couple of canoes and all our grub, since you couldn't eat the fish. The first night out, we cooked steaks over the fire. We tucked into them something good, and after, this Indian guide came over and asked could he have the bones from our steaks. There was still a lot of meat on them, we couldn't finish them .

We said yes, sure, I mean hell, what would you say? But we got thinking about it afterwards, and Charlie and I talked about it on the way home. I'd always thought of Canada as kind of a special place. Not that I knew much about it, but from what I heard, you don't have the same trouble with race and riots and poverty that you get around here. But I remember thinking after that night that maybe things weren't quite so rosy in Canada as what I'd thought.

Lawyer, Tuscaloosa, Alabama

Scenery Is Everywhere
Here, all you get are streets and streets, buildings everywhere you look, all crowded. To get any scenery, you have to go way out into the country. Up in Canada, they've got scenery everywhere.
Television Repairman, Washington, DC

A Bird In The Field Is Worth Two On The Highway
Drove up to Canada one time, just to look at the place. Along the highway, there was this big crowd, cars pulled over, regular jam-up, people all over the shoulder. Well, I pulled off, naturally, figured there was a bear or a deer or an accident or something. It was a bird, some kind of bird hopping around in a field, and everybody looking at it. I been around the world twice, been to three dog fights and a box social, but I never saw anything like that before, people lining up to gawk at a gawdamn bird.
Ranchhand, Martin City, Montana

The Hills Are Alive, I Trust?
Mountains, I think of mountains, and people singing.
Housewife, Austin, Texas

Choo Choo To You, Too
All I can think of is a railroad going through beautiful mountains. That's Canada.
Student, Boston College, Boston

It's Getting Out That's Tough
We don't hardly get but a skimmer of snow here, this is desert, it gets plenty cold, though. Up in Canada, I hear they get it all the time in the winter, you can hardly get into the house for snow.
Store Manager, McDermitt, Nevada

Come Back Next Winter
A lot of people think Canada's just a big pile of snow. Not true. I been up there, up to a place called Saskatchewan, where my daughter lives, in Regina, Saskatchewan. It's flatter'n hell and hotter'n hell, and I come from Texas.
Businessman, Waco, Texas

Mooseless and Viewless
We went up to a place near Sudbury. It was in October, and you couldn't see how pretty it was because everything was covered with snow. You couldn't see nothing. I'm used to that, in Los Angeles you can't see nothing either. It's all desert around here. We didn't get a moose, either.
Insurance adjuster, Los Angeles

Elbow Room
A really terrific country, great people, nice scenery. They've got elbow room; here, you can hardly lift a finger.
Graduate student, Yale University,
New Haven, Connecticut

73

European Accent

This summer I had occasion to go to Quebec and then down to Montreal. We didn't travel on the big highway – it's just as bad as our New York Thruway – but on the other little highway that runs along the other side of the river, and I felt there is indeed a tremendous difference between Canada and the United States. Canada is more European in character, with small farms, villages, and in Canada, the individual has a bigger role to play than here, where he just gets swallowed up in society.

Energy research company executive, Boston

The Camper Complex

The damn roads aren't done. You get on one of these run-down itty-bitty roads up there, and you get behind a trailer or a camper and you just stay there. Why don't they have interstate highways like we have? We was up there in the West, in the mountains, but all we saw was the ass-end of somebody's camper.

Lab technician, Nashville, Tennessee

Trade, Economics

Viva The Smarts
I think they're pretty damn smart. When we broke off trade relations with the Cubans back in the early '60s, the Canadians just stepped in and scooped up the business. Now they're talking about reopening negotiations with Cuba for us, but everywhere we go, we're going to be behind the Canadians in line.
Desk Officer, Commerce Department, Washington, DC

Bearding the Foe
We would get along a lot better if they didn't want to play footsie with the Cubans, going down there, this Canadian prime minister, going down to Cuba to hold Castro's hand. They can't expect us to like that.
Army Officer, Pentagon, Washington, DC

Rural Protest
Canadian farmers have been dumping their eggs on the US market. They've got a hell of a mess up there, thanks to a government egg marketing agency; they pay the farmer to produce eggs and they support the market, so they got a hell of a lot of eggs left over and they just dumped them over the border at less than the production cost. We resent this like hell; they wouldn't do this to their own farmers, undercut their prices, why should they do it to us?
Poultryman, near Ann Arbor, Michigan

Trade Warning

Goods over there are starting to deteriorate, and prices are starting to skyrocket, especially labour-wise. It's not the same ball game it was five years ago; the Canadians used to knock the stuffing out of us, but we should do a lot better now.

Clothing manufacturer, New York City

I Bet They Have A Layaway Plan

Everything's so cheap in Canada you can't hardly believe it. There is this terrific maternity shop on Bloor Street in Toronto, the Madonna or the something Madonna, and I swore if I ever got pregnant I'd go there for all my maternity clothes. Now I've gone and had a baby, and I never did get up there to get my clothes. I think it might be worth having another baby just to go up there, but my husband says no way, he doesn't want me going near the place.

Housewife, Gaffney, South Carolina

On The Right Track, Anyway

They got a first class train system up there, really first rate. The government owns the big line, the CNR, and the other big line, the CPR, has to keep up. They have an excellent safety record, they pay good money and what I hear, everybody is pretty well satisfied. I think that shows how smart the Canadians are. You wait and see, railroads are important, more important than people realize, and the Canadians are going to get the jump on us in trade, because they know it and we don't.

Conductor on the Amtrak train between Washington and New York

Not Really Foreign

Our company does a lot of work in Canada, most of the senior people around here have lived up there, one time or another, I imagine I'll go up, too, and I'm looking forward to it. Canada's like a foreign country that's not really foreign, if you know what I mean. That's one reason, I think, that so many US firms have established themselves up there. The climate is right, economics-wise, and it's the kind of place we're used to. Not like having to deal with a bunch of Arabs or that.

Of course, Canada benefits from this, from the open border, the welcome mat out for foreign capital. You can't get the capital in a country the size of Canada. You don't have a big enough market up there to justify a whole bunch of factories unless they get some help from home. We bring the capital, the experience, the good old Yankee know-how, and Canada has always been very generous, incentives and that. You can get, in some parts of the country, you can get a lot of grants, tax breaks, things like that, better than here.

Look at it this way, back in the US, you've got to be a really big company, GM, one of those, to have much clout. But up in Canada a small or medium-sized company, in American terms, is considered pretty big, gets a lot of help, a lot of tax breaks. They want us to come.

Lately, there's been some bitching, some of the nationalists aren't too happy, but that will die down. In the long run, Canadians will realize they need us as much or more than we need them.

Junior executive, pipe company, Chicago

The Investment Screen
Canada's new foreign investment screening act strikes us as a self-defeating move. As you know, Ottawa now reserves the right to allow or disallow takeovers of Canadian firms by foreign investors, for which read – let's not kid ourselves – American investors. You can understand the pressure they were under, the fuss raised by a lot of Canadian nationalists, the concern, some of it phoney, about decisions being made on matters affecting the Canadian economy without any Canadian input. But never mind why they did it, the fact is that they did it, and in our view it was a mistake. You will see a pulling back of our investment at a time when Canada needs new capital. This is not because, as you will hear some of the more berserk people around here maintain, because Canada is working up to expropriating or nationalizing foreign firms. If I were a businessman, I would have no reservations whatever about investing there, as far as the danger of expropriation or nationalization is concerned, none. At the same time, the passage of such legislation sends a signal, it tells us

77

something, whether Canadians mean it to or not. It is not exactly a welcome mat for the investor. I mean, who is going to be eager to go and face a board of inquiry before they can even put the money down? Who needs it? Besides, there aren't all that many good, solid opportunities. The Canadian economy just isn't that big.

Statistician, Department of Commerce, Washington, DC

A Word on Wheat

They got a kind of funny way of doing business up there, I know that. Here, when you take in a load of wheat to the elevator, you got no way of knowing exactly what you're going to get for it. You know in a general sort of way, but not exactly, because the price is set on the open market, what the buyers are paying for it in Minneapolis.

Up in Canada, they do it all through a wheat board, which is the government, really, although the farmers say it isn't. They know what they're going to get for the stuff before it even comes off the land. In other words, the Canadian farmer really only has one customer, and the price is set all at one time. Here, you can get a change every ten minutes or so, as the market goes up and down.

The Canadians seem to like their system, but personally, I don't, and I don't believe one farmer in ten in this area would put up with it. I don't want somebody telling me when to plant, and how much I can plant, and when I can bring it in and how much and all that. I believe in the free market system, and so do most farmers, and I believe we make more money at it than the Canadian farmers.

They may have their reasons, and I guess they do; it makes it easier for foreign trade, I guess, they have a sort of unfair advantage on us there, but I'll stick to the good old American way.

Wheat farmer near Rolla, North Dakota

A Rude Suggestion

There's your Autopact, that's Canada. Taking jobs and giving them to Canadians that we should be getting here. You can take your autopact, if you're from Canada, buddy, and stuff it up where your Granny won't see it.

Autoworker, Terre Haute, Indiana

A Political-Economic Time Lag

There is a time lag at work in Canadian-American relations. A lot of the arrangements that are in place were designed for the needs of the last generation, not the coming one. There is an assumption built in that Canada needs a helping hand from the US to straighten out its international books, so you have deals like the Defence Production Sharing Agreement, under which Canada is guaranteed the right to bid on US defence contracts on a par with any American firm, and in effect guaranteed a certain amount of the business. We wouldn't make such a deal with anybody else, and the supposition behind it is of a Canada that requires a kind of international sponsorship from this nation.

And yet, what does Canada do? You have created an air of great uncertainty. You say you will sell us your oil, you beg us to take more oil, so the quota system is revised to accommodate Canada. Nixon did that, opened up the quota. Then you say you're going to cut back on shipments of oil and natural gas at a time when they're in increasingly short supply – natural gas, especially, oil is a slightly different matter – and then, when we try to adjust to that, you say you are going to cut off our supplies altogether after a certain date, and then you change the date.

You ask us to put money into the Canadian economy so it will be developed, and we do so, for years. Not out of benevolence, nothing like that, just out of common business sense because our businessmen can see opportunities in Canada, and Canadians, who have one of the highest level of savings in the world, are not willing to put up the money to develop their own economy. So Americans more or less step in with the capital to help Canada, and then you turn around and say you don't want our damn money and you're going to cast a pretty harsh eye on any new investment, and there's a kind of knee-jerk reaction every time an American firm moves to buy out a Canadian firm, but a big hoorah goes up when a Canadian firm buys out an American firm.

So you have still got the rhetoric and the emotional outlook of a developing economy, but your economy is, in fact, highly developed. And there are a lot of arrangements between the two countries tied to that earlier outlook, tied to an attitude of dependence, almost a client state attitude. We are looking at a lot of those arrangements, and I think there are going to be some adjustments.

Staff member, Interstate and Foreign Commerce
Committee, House of Representatives, Washington, DC

Kid Brother No More

There has always been a feeling around here that Canada should be exempted from anything rough. We do something we feel we have to do to protect our trade position in the world, and then we make an exception for Canada. It goes back a long way. When Kennedy set up his Interest Equalization Tax, your people were down here right away saying "Please, sir, don't do it to us." So Canada got an exemption, and in return you agreed to keep exchange reserves up to two and a half billion dollars. That was the quid quo pro; we wouldn't hit you with the tax, and you would keep a substantial reserve so we wouldn't get clobbered with an exchange problem. But the reserve kept getting lowered and finally disappeared.

There have been a lot of things like that, special favours. Well, I think that was dumb. Canada is perfectly capable of looking after herself, perfectly able to compete with us or anybody else.

When Americans talk about the ending of the "special relationship" with Canada, that's what they mean; it's a recognition that this country will act to protect its own interests in economic matters, and if that hurts Canada as well as somebody else, well, that's too bad.

I think Canadians should be pleased; you're no longer being treated like somebody's kid brother.

Desk officer, Treasury Department, Washington, DC

The Special Relationship Again

The relationship between our two countries is so complex, so intricate, so interwoven that very little of it is covered by what would be the normal diplomatic relationship between two other countries. The normal way to do business between Canada and the US is not for our diplomats to talk to your diplomats, but for bureaucrats to talk to their opposite numbers directly, politicians to confer with other politicians directly, without the intervention of a foreign office. I doubt if our Canadian desk is aware of one per cent of the governmental traffic – I'm just talking about governmental traffic here – between the two countries. Business, travel, all those things have almost no government input at all, except in a very broad, general, background way. That's what is meant by the "special relationship" between Canada and the US and that special relationship still exists, no matter what anyone says. You can't legislate it out, you can't erase it by having an official stand up and say that it no longer exists, because it does. It is the relationship between all the intertwined parts of the Canadian government and economy with the US government and economy, the direct linkage of all the parts.

For most of the problems that come up between Canada and the US, our people don't even think of working on the Canadian-US relationship, they simply think of working on the problem. No other country in the world has that kind of relationship here.

State department officer, once on the Canada desk, Washington, DC

Faint Praise

Yes, We Have No Astronauts

I got nothing against the place, but what has Canada ever done? You never hear "Canadian Astronaut Lands On Moon," do you? No, really, do you? Or Canadian-Russian troops clash, or Canada invents new medical miracle, no, really, do you? So, what kind of place is it?

National Guardsman, Cleveland, Ohio

The Unturned Applecarts

I married a Canadian, and I've spent a lot of time in Canada, so I think I know something about Canadians, but not really. I mean, I think of them in a whole series of contradictions.

They're militant and refreshing, most of the time, but they are not outraged when things are bad. They tend to put up with things that Americans would raise hell over. They don't ever want to take chances, but that doesn't stop them complaining about people who do take chances and wind up owning their resources.

They don't seem willing to act on their own convictions, but that doesn't stop them from having all sorts of convictions. They're money conscious, but they claim not to be . . .

Don't get me wrong, I like Canadians, but I don't think a lot of them work hard enough for the kind of salaries they demand . . .

They never want to upset the applecart, they are seldom assertive or inventive, but that doesn't prevent them bitching about other people. . . They are willing to pay other people to come in and walk away with their own property. They say, "The damn Americans are buying up our country," instead of "Us damn Canadians are selling out our country." Canadians aren't secure enough in themselves to stand self-criticism, so they direct it all at somebody else – preferably the government. They're generous enough, and willing to spend money, but on the wrong things . . . They spend it on somebody else coming into the country, instead of spending it for their own benefit. I think they voted for Trudeau because he lets them go on dreaming instead of getting to work. The way their government is set up, they feel they have no control, but it's not true, and they should wise up.

High school teacher, Pocatela, Idaho

So What Have You Got Against Paraguay?

No, we don't teach Canadian history. Well, we do a bit, up until the War of 1812, and after that, we just let it go. I suppose we should teach it. History is interesting, you can learn from the history of any nation, but teaching Canadian history here would be like teaching the history of Paraguay. Interesting, but not important.

Junior high school history teacher, New York City

Or, Failing That, Toronto?

Canada's such a terrific place, I'd move there tomorrow if I could. I'd go anywhere, even Nova Scotia.

Legal secretary, Gastonia, North Carolina

Trampled Feelings

We were assigned up in Canada for a while, my wife and I and the kids. To tell you the truth, we didn't like it much. When our kids went to school, they were subjected to a lot of anti-American propaganda. Do you know, they had to look at the Viet Cong and Red Chinese flags in school? It seemed to me the over-riding motive was to trample on our feelings.

Auto company executive, Cleveland, Ohio

83

Well, Brains Ain't Everything
Nice people, very nice. Not bright, but nice.
Tractor salesman, Fargo, North Dakota

Every Boost A Knock
You never hear anything bad about Canada, that's one thing. In fact, I guess it's the only thing.
English major, University of Indiana, Bloomington

Yeah, But We're Tubby
It's a big place, bigger than the United States. Don't seem right, somehow, for the itty-bitty number of people they got up there.
Housewife, Hartford, Connecticut

You Can't Win 'Em All
It isn't your fault you're Canadians. You could have been Americans if you'd been lucky and joined the Revolution in 1776. That's the attitude here. It's a pretty cruddy, patronizing attitude, but there it is.
Book salesman, Denver, Colorado

An Inferiority Complex
They're doing some very exciting things in teaching, in education generally. I admire the OISE (Ontario Institute for Studies in Education) in Toronto, they're doing some very advanced work there. But here's a funny thing. There is a feeling that what is done in Canada somehow isn't as good as what is done in the US. I teach education, and I can't find where the feeling is justified, but there's no doubt it exists and it has a spillover effect down here so that American intellectuals who take positions in Canada are somewhat apologetic about going, as if they were taking up a second-class post.
Education lecturer, Harvard, Cambridge, Massachusetts

Mediocrity

They have a pretty good school system. Canadian universities are cheaper than they are down here, and they will accept American students readily. There has been a pretty fair migration of our students up north, which is fairly recent. It used to go pretty much the other way. I think it's a good thing, although I'm not sure if I were a really brilliant student I'd want to go up there. Canadian universities are never as bad as the worst American universities, but they're never as good as the really excellent ones in this country.

Harvard University lecturer, Cambridge, Massachusetts

Psst, Wanna Hear A Secret? No.

Canada can afford the luxury of straight dealing. In this country, the decisions in foreign policy are always made covertly. There is the notion that everything should give way to national security, whatever that is, everything should be left up to the Secretary of State, he knows all, sees all, but he can't tell all because the Russians might be listening. In Canada, there are no defence secrets to defend. At least if there are any secrets, nobody cares.

Radio news reporter, Pittsburgh

Getting Along (Mainly) Like a House on Fire: 1897-1916

Of Course I'll Respect You After: 1918-60

The early part of this century was marked by increasing cross-border chumminess, and reciprocity was revived. Unfortunately, it appeared that many Americans coveted our land more than our trade, and Champ Clark's ill-timed 1911 speech – I have quoted the crucial section – helped wreck not only reciprocity, but Wilfrid Laurier's chances in the 1911 election. Our passion faded, and soon we were quarrelling bitterly over US reluctance to enter World War I (a reluctance shared by some Canadians, especially in Quebec). Then they were calling us a country without a soul.

December 27, 1897: Canada, a Married Flirt

[The British diplomats] avow their slavery to Canadians and chafe under it, and yet they rather resent our talking to Canada directly . . . It is far more to Canada's advantage than to ours to be on good terms with us. Lord Salisbury, in a private conversation the other day, compared her to a coquettish girl with two suitors, playing off one against the other. I should think a closer analogy would be to call her a married flirt, ready to betray John Bull on any occasion, but holding him responsible for all her follies.

John Hay, US ambassador to Great Britain

July 28, 1903: How We Bullied Britain

The fact is England cares nothing about the boundary, but their fear of offending the Canadians is something inconceivable. That collection of bumptious provincials bullies them to an extent and they dare not say a word.

Henry Cabot Lodge, who was an American nominee on the commission set up to settle the Alaskan Boundary dispute. Bullies or not, we got skinned alive in the settlement.

1904: Good Poet, Bum Prophet

Long ere the second Centennial arrives, there will be fifty great states, among them Canada and Cuba.

Walt Whitman, in a letter from Canada

JOHN BULL: "Yes, 'e's makin' a lot of noise, Sam, but 'e'll get over it." – From the *North American* (Philadelphia)

1911: Reciprocity Unsheathed
Canadian annexation is the logical conclusion of reciprocity with Canada.

Senator P. J. McCumber, in debate

1911: We Don't Grant Favours, We Bestow Them
We need Canada more than she needs us. In a few years we shall have to beg for favours that now she might willingly grant.

Eugene Foss, campaigning for reciprocity in Massachusetts

1911: The Velvet Glove ...
The United States recognizes that the Dominion of Canada is a permanent North American political unit and that her autonomy is secure ... There is not the slightest probability that their racial and moral union will involve any political change, or annexation, or absorption.

Philander Chase Knox, Secretary of State

1911: . . . And The Iron Fist
Be not deceived, when we go into a country and get
control of it, we take it.
Congressman G. W. Prince of Illinois

February 14, 1911: Champ Clark Among the Igloos
I am for [reciprocity] because I hope to see the day when the
American flag will float over every square foot of the British
North American possessions clear to the North Pole. They are
people of our blood. They speak our language. Their
institutions are much like ours . . . I do not have any doubt
whatever that the day is not far distant when Great Britain will
joyfully see all her North American possessions become a part
of this Republic. That is the way things are tending now.
Representative Champ Clark of Missouri, in debate

February 11, 1915: Endorsement from a Satisfied Customer
I have lived in Canada in the summer time for thirteen years out
of [the last] twenty-two. I have an intense interest in your
development, profound confidence in the great future of your
Dominion, and great admiration for the policy of the Mother
Country in lightening the bonds that unite you to the Empire.
*William Howard Taft, in a Toronto speech (He was no longer
president.)*

1916: Say It Isn't So
Canada is a country without a soul.
**Unnamed American, quoted by Rupert Brooke in
Letters from America**

The period from 1918 to the early 1960s was marked by the stupendous growth of American investment in Canada, its uncritical acceptance in this country, and the emergence of our "special relationship" with the United States. I have skipped lightly through the – mainly banal – comments of the time, and singled out only some typical passages, and one dissenting view from the US side. The assumption of these years, on both sides of the border, was that Canada belonged firmly in the US ambit, and continentalism was much applauded by most of us, and almost all of them.

April 12, 1918: Oh, Brother

For over a hundred years these two peoples have lived in peace and happiness as close neighbours, settling such questions as have naturally arisen in an orderly and friendly manner. This is very significant. Does it not point to the fact that in ideals and aims these two great people are alike? Does it not suggest that they are brothers in spirit, whatever the genealogist may say? I like to feel that it does, and I know my fellow-countrymen generally share that view.

John D. Rockefeller, Jr., in a Montreal speech

1926: Fallout from a Freebee

In 1926, the Canadian government laid on a trip through western Canada for a number of US editors and writers (such trips are still run, in a valiant but vain effort to dispel American ignorance about us). Two typical comments from the travelling journalists follow.

The visitor to Western Canada will find the people friendly and hospitable. The settler will find the pep and neighbourliness that is characteristic of a young country. There is little in Winnipeg or Calgary that is different from Bloomington or Des Moines. The policemen are typical English "Bobbies," it is true, and a Mac on the front of your name is an advantage. There is Irish laughter in the eyes of clerks and waitresses.

C. V. Gregory, Editor, the Prairie Farmer

Perhaps the most pronounced impression that I got on my recent trip through Western Canada was that of the bigness of the country. My conception of a fringe of agricultural lands along our

Northern border and above that a vast area of snow and ice had to be revised. At Edmonton, over three hundred miles from our border, we were in the midst of some of the best agricultural lands I ever saw, and we found a people prospering in a big way at farming and stock-raising. Yet we were told by people who know that there was a farming country just as fine three hundred miles further north, on the Peace River.

Coming from the South, it was a surprise to me, though it should not have been so, to find that among our numerous hosts in the many communities we visited in Western Canada were the names I am used to hearing down home every day. Some of the people had English names, some Scotch, some Irish and some hailed from the Continent, or their ancestors did. Some of the citizens had been born there, more had come from the Eastern part of the country, some from the Motherland and many from down in the States. And the resulting whole was as fine a citizenship as any country in the world can boast of. The people I ran into in Western Canada are just the kind of neighbours we would like to have.

L. R. Neel, the Southern Agriculturalist

August 9, 1929: The Beer, at Least, is Real
I also went to Canada. Montreal is four-fifths imitation American and one-fifth imitation English – but the beer and ale were splendidly real.

Thomas Wolfe, novelist, in a letter

September, 1933: Pointing the Way, Together
I place great emphasis on the importance of close co-operation between Canada and the United States. Our point of view is much the same, unhandicapped by prejudices and hatreds. Our task of closer co-operation is not as difficult as in other parts of the world: a leadership in international co-operation should come from us.

Averell Harriman, at a Liberal Conference in Port Hope, Ontario

I WANT YOU

1940: The Ties That Bind
The real reason for Canada's tardy growth is to be found partly in her spiritual dependence on Great Britain, which has often paralyzed her energies, but to a far greater extent in her geographical proximity to the United States.
John MacCormac of the New York Times, in
Canada, America's Problem

1948: An Offer We Couldn't Refuse, But Did
Canadians are the closest friends we have in the world, and they are in serious economic trouble. From the US, they need and deserve considerably less apathy about their plight. More than that, they need complete and permanent economic union with the US . . . since Canada has shown that she cannot operate fiscally in today's world. It is up to the US to act.
An editorial in Life *magazine*

1952: Step Outside And Say That, Bye
[Newfoundlanders] are so inbred as to be half-witted.
Col. Robert McCormick, Chicago publisher,
after a visit to Canada

1960: Buddy, Can You Spare A Dime?
I have always gotten along with the Canadians until they put the extra ten cents on the dollar. I did not like that.
Representative Clare Hoffman of Michigan

1960: Psst, The Border's Invisible – Tell The Customs Guy
I cannot really see any difference between Canadians and citizens of the United States. To all intents and purposes we are one. The boundary-line is imaginary.
Senator Irving Ives of New York, quoted in
James M. Minife's Peacemaker or Powder-Monkey

The Undefended Border

But Who's Steering?
I just feel as if Canadians are our brothers and sisters.
I feel that Canada and the US are one as far as I'm
concerned. We're both in the same boat; not in all
respects, but in most.
Retired businessman, Grand Rapids, Michigan

Fetch My Water-wings
I have a swimming pool out in my backyard, and I have a
fourteen-year-old daughter. When she was just a little girl, we
used to go swimming together a lot, and she would put her
arms around my neck and we would swim along just fine. But
now, if she puts her arms around my neck, we both sink,
because she is much bigger. And what is happening today is
that Canada is still clinging onto the neck of the United States
long after it was time to let go. You have the sixth largest
resource and economic base in the world, you have a highly
educated work force, lots of capital, and more resources than
you have yet been able to put to work, and yet your people are
down here all the time asking for special favours from us, and
giving up nothing in return.

I just don't think it's going to go on like that, I think the
days of clinging to Uncle Sam's back are over.
Official in the Finance Branch,
Treasury Department, Washington, DC

Power To Which People?
I don't think there is much doubt that one day electric power is
going to be used from Canada to light New York City. If there
still is a New York City. That's just one example of the way our
two countries are intermingled. There are some irritations on
both sides of the border. We think Canadians are too quick to
criticize and too slow to jump in and help out. They think we're
too aggressive and pushy. We get sore because Canadians seem to
be willing to accept our investment capital and yet resent our
control on the financial side – which naturally goes with
investment capital. But these things can be worked out, the
irritations are temporary, but the friendship is permanent.
Power company officer, Buffalo, New York

A Pity
I see it as a place with a whole different way of life. The people
are the same, but they aren't so pushy, so hassled, and they
don't get on each other all the time the way we do down here.
My Dad was in the services and we were stationed in a lot of
different places. We were stationed up near eastern Canada for
a while, and at school I heard a little bit about it. Not much,
the usual stuff about Mounties and Eskimos and wide open
spaces. Anyway, I used to ask my Dad why we were never
stationed in Canada, and he used to tell me it was a different
country and didn't belong to us, and I always thought that was
a pity and I still do.
Shipping clerk, Albuquerque, New Mexico

Where's the Difference?
I can't see much difference between the two countries,
know what I mean? In my business it's the same thing
in Toledo or Toronto or Windsor or Detroit. When the
same people do the work, they're going to be even
more the same. Where's the difference?
Tool and dye maker, Toledo, Ohio

Pushing Back On The Fish Front
They's good fishermen, that's for sure. They know what to do
with a net and a boat. Sometimes they's pushy, that's okay, we
pushes back.
Fisherman, Ocean Point, Maine

An Udder View
We share this continent with two other nations, Mexico and
Canada. Around this part you hear something about Mexico,
especially about whether we can persuade the Mexicans to give us
some of their water, but you hear very little about Canada,
although there was some talk for a while of trying to get more
natural gas from up north. You get the impression – at least, I get
the impression – that the United States regards these other
nations as a milk cow to be used for our benefit. This is something
that, if I were a Canadian, would worry me quite a bit.
Astronomy student, University of Arizona

Who's To Know?
You take your average Canadian and your average American
he's just about the same, am I right? Short, tall, round, fat or
whatever, who's to know which is which, am I right? They got a
lot in common, a man that comes from a big Canadian city or a
big American city they're a lot alike, more than a guy comes from
a big Canadian city and another from a small Canadian town,
am I right? A city's a city. But it's different. Your Canadian
comes from a different background in some ways, am I right? You
got your royalty, frankly I don't think that matters a damn, who
pays any attention nowadays, but there's a difference. You got
other things, too, political things, and you got in some ways a
different approach. I'm not saying it's better and I'm not saying
it's worse, am I right? It's just different. Your American is more
individualistic-oriented, am I right? In the service we had a guy
from Canada, New Brunswick or one of those cities, and he
wouldn't say shit if his mouth was full of it. The way I saw it, he
was always looking for someone to tell him what to do. So that's
on the one hand. On the other hand, you don't see Canadians in
the kind of mess you got down East, in New York, Boston, places
like that, Detroit, Chicago and that. That's why I came out here
from Detroit. You don't get that in Canada, so maybe one thing
goes with the other, and who's to say which is better, Canada or
the US. I don't know, am I right?
Mechanic, Des Moines, Iowa

An Invitation To Sign Up
I've never been able to see the sense of a border between the
two countries at all to tell the truth. There are so many things

in which Canadians and Americans are alike that things where they're different don't amount to a hill of beans. We speak the same language, watch the same TV, come from the same background, not entirely, I mean, but generally. So what's the big deal? Take my business, I'm in paper. Most of the paper here comes from Canada, did you know that? So what happens? They grow the trees in Canada and ship them down here and we make them into paper and send the paper back, which it costs more in Canada than it does in the United States. And for why? Because of the tariff, that's why. What's the point of that? I mean, why should Canadians pay more for their own stuff than we do, just because there's a border? I don't think people up there understand these things. I think if most Canadians knew what the politicians were up to, they'd say to hell with it, and join the good old USA.

Paper Salesman, Gary, Indiana

Close, But No Cigar

Your president's wife just had a nervous breakdown, didn't she?

Math student, University of Hawaii, Honolulu

Travellers

The Celsius Difference

I've never felt alien in Canada, it's just a place like home. I mean, if you go to a big Canadian city, it's like going to a big American city. But the last time I went to Toronto, we flew in and I got into the airport limousine to go downtown, and we were going along the lakefront there, and there's this big sign that gives the time and temperature. This was an evening in September, and it said 12 degrees, and the time was 21:37. It was Celsius, in Canada, they give the temperature in Celsius now, and the time was on the 24-hour clock. I thought that was kind of nice. It let you know you were in a different country, and everything isn't exactly the same.

Salesman, New York City

You Could Check His Birth Certificate

The only way I know to tell a Canadian from an American is to go outside and look at his licence plate. That's the only difference there is.

General store manager, Barr, Montana

Grab Yes, Tip No

Same as everyone else, filthy the place up, drink too much, grab your ass if they can get it, and don't leave a tip.

Chambermaid, Port Jervis, New York

You're Welcome
Canadians are ever so interesting, just fascinating people. We get
a lot of them down here, of course, lot of people from Vancouver,
but other Canadian cities, too, Montreal, Toronto, Winnipeg,
come down here on vacation. They're very polite, come in, sign
the register – a lot of people don't sign the register – and we
answer any questions, and they're real friendly. Maybe you get a
better class of people when they travel, maybe all Canadians
aren't like that, I'm not saying, but they seem real interested in
the history of San Francisco. And they always say, "Thank you."
Tourist guide, San Francisco

In A Restaurant, Tucker, Georgia
"Yew cain't hardly unnerstan' what Canadians say, the way they
tawk."
"What do you mean?"
"They tawk funny, sorta mumbly an' ah donno whatall. Yew
cain't harly make 'em aout."
"Am I doing it now?"
"Yessir, yew surely ahr."

Well, I've Had A Cold Lately
**That's funny, you don't sound Canadian. Canadians all
sound French.**
Waitress, Philadelphia, Pennsylvania

Nothing But The Truth (Or Consequences)
We don't get but a few Canadians down here, and most of
them are just travelling through. They see the sign for the town
on the highway and come on in. That's why we called the place
Truth Or Consequences. Ralph Edwards [former master of
ceremonies for the TV program] come down here one time and
told us if we'd change the name from Hot Springs he'd give us
a whole lot of publicity on his show, so they took a vote on it
and they did her. So that's why we see Canadians, they come
in for the sign and of course there's a few lives here and
married to Americans. We can't tell any difference between
Canadians and Americans. They're all about alike to us, and

we judge people by what they're like and not where they come from or who their Daddy was, and we find it works out a whole lot better that way.

Garage operator, Truth Or Consequences, New Mexico

Aw, Come On, Nobody's The Same In Ohio

Canadians, Americans, they're no different. As far as I can see, nobody's different, not even in Ohio. We've got a place there, too.

Hotel owner, Marathon, Florida

The Canadian Shield

People forget that if this country comes under attack, it will be from the North, right over the Pole, right through Canada. I think we should be very careful to cultivate stronger ties with Canadians instead of all these recriminations that's going on and you keep reading about in the paper. The time is maybe going to come when we need those people.

Barber, Pittsburgh, Pennsylvania

A Word From Our Sponsor

I've never had the pleasure of visiting Canada, but everything I've heard about it, it's really good. All I know about it what you see on the TV, the ads, where they say there's a lot to see. I'm sure that's right.

Postal clerk, McAlister, Alabama

Polite Police

They've got a much better court system, much better police, too. Around here, the courts are all loaded against the poor and the kids. If your old man's a big shot, you can get away with murder. And the lawyers, they won't do a thing for you without you got money. It stinks.

One time my friend he was up in Toronto, and he was on the street just sort of standing around, you know, like downtown, standing around and there were quite a few people standing around and all of a sudden up comes a police car and this cop gets out and he says "I wonder if you would mind breaking it up, holding your little meeting someplace else." Something like that, I don't know the exact words. He says, "We've had a complaint, some of the neighbours, and could you just cool it." And then everybody started to move away and this cop he comes around to get into his car and he bumps into my friend, he says "Excuse me, sir." Excuse me! Christ, my friend nearly crapped. This was a white cop, too.

Labourer, Cincinnati, Ohio

A Bust
A friend of mine just wrote me from Canada. He was riding on the train and the cops came on board at Saskatoon and busted him for carrying dope. It was quite illegal the way they did it. He spent one night in jail and that's all, but you wonder about the cops up there. He has long hair, that's the only reason they picked him out to search.

Political science student, Yale University

No Hassles
I was brought up in the North – Bangor, Maine – trees, hunting and all that. I worked as a lumberman, fisherman, you name it . . . We used to go up to Calais, that's not much more than a hundred miles, and over to Canada. We used to go across the border all the time, and it wasn't no different. My uncle worked in a spinning mill up there, in Calais, and the mill went right across the river. At one end you were in Canada and at the other you were in the good old USA. And it was exactly the same. We used to go up to Millwood Bridge and go back and forth across the border. I liked the way people got along. There were no hassles. You take a guy from Calais, Maine and a guy from St. Stephen, New Brunswick, just on the other side, and they are as like as peas in a pod . . . You take a guy from Calais and a guy from New York, now, they're miles apart, worlds apart, know what I mean? So what I say, the difference between Canadians and Americans has a lot more to do with what part of the country they come from than which country they come from. A city boy in Canada and a city boy in the US – no different. A Maritime boy and a down-easter, no different. But a guy from Montreal and a Kansas

farmer, hell, yes, they see the world through different eyes. That's all it is.

I always felt strongly about this, about Canadians and Americans being the same. During the war, I was in the Special Forces, Canadian and American, remember them? We even had two arm flashes, showing we were international and mixed up Canadians and Americans.

There's different politics and that, and different leaders, but as far as I'm concerned, I was in the Special Forces for a reason, and the reason is, Canadians, Americans, they're about the same to me.

Security guard, Hamden, Connecticut

Holier Than Thou

The Canadians have adopted a holier-than-thou attitude which is singularly misapplied. They are very quick to criticize us for Watergate, for the state of our cities, for racial problems. They seem to think they are more moral than we are. But they have had political scandals, too. I was listening to the CBC the other day, and they were talking about the Mirabel airport, outside Montreal. The same kind of payoffs and things were going on there as you see down here. So I don't buy the superiority of Canadian morals. As for race, they have problems, too. They changed their immigration laws to keep out blacks, only they didn't admit it, they said it had nothing to do with race. But it did. The atmosphere and the attitude wasn't a whole lot different than you'd find in Detroit.

Immigration officer, Detroit

The Fish of Progress

Canadians have put more effort into the Great Lakes clean-up than we have, anybody can see that. That has led them to criticize us and perhaps it was justified. They say they're nearly finished the job we both undertook to do in 1972, while we've hardly started. Well, that's right. We won't catch up until at least 1978. At the same time, we have started to move, and what we have done has, for example, started to bring the fish back to Lake Erie. That's progress, and we hope our Canadian friends understand that we are trying to do our best to make more progress.

Environmental Protection Agency official, Cleveland, Ohio

Wait'll You Hear About The Large-Mouth Bass
I hear it's real nice, a nice place. I hear the fishing's
really good, trout and that. That's all I know.
Parking lot attendant, Denver, Colorado

Hammer-proof
I love Canada, really do, and when I hear reports that there seems
to be some sort of rift between the US and Canada, it really
upsets me. I view Canadians as Americans, or if you like you can
view me as a Canadian who happens to live in Michigan. Why? It
comes from my background, I guess. In school we were always
told that Canadians are our greatest friends, our loyal friends and
that is the simple truth.

Canadians and Americans, you can't separate them with a
sledge-hammer.
Political reporter, Grand Rapids, Michigan

Say Hello To Aunt Minnie
We're really ignorant about Canada, even though we shouldn't
be. It's like Aunt Minnie in Australia; you know she's your aunt,
and you know you're connected to her, you know you should be
interested in her welfare, but when you get right down to it, who
really cares?
Manufacturers' agent, Denver, Colorado

Sporting Life

Everybody's A Specialist
Canadians do some things very well, know what I mean, and other things not so hot and some things not at all. You take hockey, Canadians can really play hockey. When the Rangers were up on top, it was all Canadians, whether it was your Andy Bathgate or whoever, they wasn't hardly any Americans in the game and they still ain't. But you take your baseball, shit, Canada isn't even in it. You got Montreal Expos, yeah, but a Canadian couldn't get on the team without he showed his passport, know what I mean? Your football, same thing, who the hell ever heard of a Canadian football player?

I don't know why it is they should be so good at hockey and not them other things. Only thing I figure is, it's so frigging cold up there, they gotta play hockey all the time to keep warm.

Cab driver, New York City

On Track
They ski a lot, I know that.
University of Iowa student, Iowa City

Moose Juice?
I was only up there once, moose hunting. I remember it as kind of a wild place. Everything wild, the people, too. Of course, I was drunk most of the time, so maybe that isn't fair.
Appliance clerk, Dover, Delaware

Well, We're Rough Diamonds, That's All
Some guys up in Canada going to buy the San Francisco
Giants I hear, heard it on the TV. What a laugh. Baseball up in
Canada, can you imagine it, guys running across the ice with a
baseball bat, don't make me cry. What the hell does Canada
know about baseball? Do we try to teach them hockey? No, no
more than the Russians. Canadians, Russians, they play good
hockey, they're used to it. But baseball, don't make me cry.
Trouble with Canada is, they want to play with the big boys,
and they get in over their head. It was the same thing with this
football deal, you know, the World Football League thing.
That guy from Toronto with all the dough, he got mixed up in
it, and he was going to fix everything up, hired all those guys,
Czonka, Kiick, all those guys from Miami, gave them these big
contracts and then what happened? Nothing, that's what
happened. Because he was out of his league, didn't know his
ass from centre field. And what happened? Whole thing went
up the flue is what happened, all that money spent and nothing
to show for it but a lot of rich lawyers. It'll be the same here,
you see. Baseball. Christ. That's big business, big American
business. I got nothing against Canadians, far as I know
they're fine people, polite, I hear, but they better stick to what
they know. Which is hockey, sure as hell not baseball.
Salesman, Cincinnati, Ohio

**With Only Three Downs, You Gotta Make
Allowances**
They play crappy football, that's all I can tell you.
Furniture dealer, Harrisburg, Pennsylvania

Would You Believe A Large Dog?
I'll tell you one thing about Canadians surprised me. They ride
well, bloody well. You see them on television, the jumping meets,
you see Canadians doing well, real well, almost every time. That
surprised me, I don't know why, I just don't think of Canadians
as anybody who is going to ride a horse.
Student, City College, New York

POLITICS IN SPORTS

TRUDEAU'S FINAL POSITION

" LET THE FESTIVITIES BEGIN !"

Hy Rosen - Albany, New York Times-Union

Taiwan or Not Taiwan
What Canada did to Taiwan, that Olympics thing, that was
cheesy. They said they could participate and then they wouldn't
let them in. Banana republic stuff.
State Legislator, Zanesville, Ohio

I was rather bemused with all the fuss over Taiwan and the
Olympics. Canada was being accused of bringing politics into the
games, as if there hadn't been politics in the games from the very
beginning. The Canadian position made sense, if you ask me, but
the jocks ran away with it down here, and a lot of crap got
written.
Law teacher, Case Western Reserve University,
Cleveland, Ohio

The Happy Ending, Of Course
To me, Canada is Barbara Ann Scott, whirling around
on the ice, so pretty, winning all those medals. And
then she married an American, of course, and moved
to Chicago. Isn't that sweet?
Office clerk, Grand Rapids, Michigan

Sw-e-e-e-p!

They got a game up there, you ever hear of it, called curling? You have this big stone and you throw it down the ice, like bowling, really more like lawn bowling, and these other people standing around have brooms and they brush the living shit out of the ice and that's the way it's played. I saw it on the television one time. It's practically a national sport the way the guy explained it, and he said they used to play it with jam pots. What the hell? They say you can tell a lot about people by the sport, you know, they reflect what they feel in the sports they pick. Well, all I got to say is every time I think of Canada I think of these poor, dumb bastards flailing away with a broom while a rock goes whizzing by.

Hardware clerk, Cape Charles, Virginia

Defending
the Border

The Apple Barricade

Americans have traditionally thought of themselves as belonging to one of the strongest, most powerful and most affluent nations in the history of the world, and they think of Canada as a simple, good neighbour, being very much smaller, very much less affluent, very much less powerful. They think of Canada as a sort of appendage which Americans have always taken for granted with a certain, not exactly condescending attitude so much as a feeling that Americans will set their policies and Canada will fit their policies to that.

They don't understand the reaction of Canadians to this attitude, which is a high degree of sensitivity which has given rise to a new nationalism in that country, reflected in many ways, political and economic.

Canadians see themselves as sleeping with an elephant, and they don't like the sensation, and Americans don't understand why ... In my own district, you get some bizarre things. I was asked to intervene because some apples from the State of Washington had been sent up to Canada to be placed in cold storage, and then when we wanted to get them back, there was a problem at the border. Our customs people didn't want to let them in ... It takes something like that to remind us that there is a border, sometimes ...

These things are not serious, in the long run they will fade away, but they are bound to come up from time to time for the very reason I have given – that we, Americans and Canadians, see ourselves in entirely different lights.

Congressman, State of Washington

A Beef

Ask me, Canadians are very selfish kinda people. They got some tariffs that go up and down like a toilet seat and to hell with anyone else. They put an embargo on beef shipments to Canada, at the same time they were dumping eggs over here and I don't call that right. The beef thing was a farce, start to finish. They kept saying it was because of the DES [a tenderizing enzyme legal in the US but banned in Canada for some time; recently, a move to ban it in the US has begun]. DES didn't have shit to do with it. You could check that out, you could get a check that there wasn't any DES in the stuff going to Canada, simple as that, all you need is a certificate from a vet. It was the price they were after. Our beef was cheaper, and Canadians wanted to buy it. We wanted to sell it, too. We were hurting. But they said no. They said, "To hell with you, the American beef producer." Well, Canada has been in trouble and we always helped out in the past. I'm not sure we will be so fast to help in the future.

Cattleman near Madison, Wisconsin

Autopact Blues

Some time ago, I forget the exact time, the Canadians came down here with a complaint about their car business. They said they were having a hell of a time and it was all our fault, American cars were being shipped into Canada and taking up the market. Maybe it was true, I guess it was, but I tell you the answer was a hell of a lot worse than the disease. That was the Autopact, and the deal was that a certain number of cars had to be built in Canada and there was a minimum in there and you couldn't go below that minimum and the theory was that way there would be a fair share of the market for Canadians. Well, hell, by the time they got screwing around with it, they got it screwed up so good that everybody was worrying about the Canadian worker and nobody gave a damn for the American worker and when things got bad here a while back and the ass end went out of the market, you had the situation where Canada was guaranteed a certain number of cars every year, but not us. You had Canadian guys pulling down good money while our guys were sitting on their asses sucking wind. We tried to get something done about it, but no way. The companies were happy, you know how these big companies work, they just shift stuff around till they get the stuff cheapest and rake in the dough and that was in Canada.

If you ask me, they should scrap the Autopact and try again and this time not buy any crap about "I'm a Canadian, look at me, I'm just a poor little guy."

Autoworker, Gary, Indiana

Trouble Comes Naturally
Trouble is bound to be part of our relationship, trouble comes naturally to two tough, independent friends. We should work to fix our problems, not be surprised that we have them.

Congressional aide, Washington, DC

I Wish I Was A Canadian
Canadians don't know how lucky they are. You've got a political system that works, not everybody's a crook, you don't go around shooting everybody, holding up banks and all that. I wish to God I was a Canadian, I'd never walk across the border again.

Store clerk, Arlington, Virginia

We Should Blush

Don't Forget Smart
I think of simplicity, naturalness, ruggedness. It's wholesome, unsophisticated, vigorous and beautiful.
Minister, Grand Rapids, Michigan

The Sweden of North America
I think Canadians are accorded a certain level of political purity here by left-wing and radical students because they're not part of the American mess. This gives them a certain cachet whenever there is a political discussion. I mean, they weren't part of the war in Vietnam, and it was a haven for the guys who fled the draft, so Canada is kind of the Sweden of North America.
Graduate student, Harvard University

We Stand On Guard For Whom?
There was a hell of a fuss a while back about the way draft dodgers were going up to Canada and deserters and so forth and the Canadian government was taking them in and sheltering them. What people forgot was that about twice as many Canadians were down here and enlisted to go and fight in Vietnam as Americans deserted up there, and I think if Canada is going to get criticized for helping the draft dodgers, she should get credit for helping to fight the war, too.
Army Captain, Waco, Texas

An Eye-Opener

I go up to Toronto a lot. I've been there six times in the last twenty-five years and I think it's a beautiful place, but the last time I was there I was really impressed . . . I'm a social worker, I do a lot of work with people in low-income housing, and the Ontario program was an eye-opener. In New York, the poor are hived off in dirty little ghettos, and the subsidized housing is crappy and dirty and the maintenance is lousy. In Toronto, public housing is spread around, not in a ghetto, and the buildings are well designed, well kept up and it's really very impressive and a credit to Canadians.

Social worker, New York City

A Friendly, Green Place

I have a concept of Canada as a very beautiful country, very cold in places, with population pockets here and there, but mostly unpopulated. For about five years I've had this dream of riding the trans-Canada railway from coast to coast, but the closest I got was to go to Montreal for two days and I spent the entire time in a friend's apartment, working on a film. Just the same, that's how I remember it, a wide, friendly, green place.

Businesswoman, East Holden, Maine

To See A Maple, Maybe?

It's one of those places I always kind of wanted to go to, but I could never figure out any reason why I should.

Secretary, Williamsburgh, Virginia

Mystic Maples

I think every American dreams of having a tract of land in Canada where he could retire and retreat from the world. A mythology of the frontier. Around the table in a saloon, you'll hear people talking about having a hunting lodge in Canada or a farm up in the Canadian hills. There's a mysticism, the cleanness, the wide expanses.

Store manager, Hays, Kansas

Waltons North
I think of Canada as a cute little place, women in long dresses, men in hats. Sort of like the Waltons on TV.
Restaurant hostess, Phoenix, Arizona

Dreams and Dross
There is a dreamlike quality about Canada, the place you want to go to, the ultimate, perfect place, the place invented by God for Americans to emulate and look up to. That's the one thing I can say about it. In reality, Canada's probably just as shitty as any place else, but if that's the case, I don't want to know about it.
Student, University of Colorado, Boulder

The Future Belongs ...
I see it as a land of tremendous possibilities, tremendously exciting. It's like America in its pioneer days, I don't mean in the technology, I mean that the land is underpopulated, full of resources, with an enormous development potential. When I have been there, I have been very much reminded of Australia, for the same reason. A land of the future, no question about that.
Physics professor, University of Arizona, Tucson

Who Are These Guys Anyway?: 1960-1974

In recent years, Canadian-American relations have gone through some abrupt sea-changes. Canadians, even those who were not fond of John Diefenbaker, resented US interference during the 1963 election, when we got into a battle over the Canadian acceptance of American nuclear arms. We became broody and unpredictable; the lessons of Walter Gordon's 1957 Royal Commission on Canada's Economic Prospects were beginning to percolate through public consciousness, and we began to wonder whether out ties with the US had not grown too close. Americans responded – still respond – with bewilderment, hurt, occasional querulousness, enormous goodwill, and unplumbable ignorance.

January 17, 1963: Ottawa is not Oxford, Miss.

President Kennedy, Secretary of State Dean Rusk and Defence Secretary Robert S. McNamara, all but hung in effigy here, led with their chins in the Canadian affair [the battle over nuclear arms]. They forgot Canada is not US Steel and Roger Blough, and that Ottawa is not Oxford, Mississippi.

Canada, unified shortly after our own Civil War (1867), is nearly half the size of the Soviet Union. This remarkable nation is eighth in the world's manufacturing and fifth in world trade – surpassed only by the United States, Great Britain, France and Japan. Quite a record for about as many people as live in our single state of New York. Moreover, their land-handy market is America's largest export customer.

For fifteen years we've given billions away abroad each year and charged it to our taxpayers. That doesn't go for Canada. She has never accepted a nickel in gifts from the United States. How many countries in the entire world can say that?

. . . There is a place for diplomacy in our troubled world and one of its chief purposes is to inspirit our allies. Yet each failure to do this somehow increases the New Frontiersmen's arrogant flash of their intellectual monocles. If this goes on long enough, or our money runs out, we won't have a friend left.

Henry Taylor, Washington Daily News

February 9, 1963: Put Up Your Nukes
It is stating the obvious to say that Canada has been sweeping the
nuclear issue under the rug because of a considerable body of
opinion in Canada which shuns nuclear war and nuclear
weapons. We have the right and the obligation to our citizens to
find out without delay whether Canada intends to finish the joint
defence arrangements she began with us in 1958. Canada must be
advised along with many others of our western allies that the US
can no longer afford to furnish them the protection of our
military strength while they decline, for domestic political reasons
or any other, to fulfil their obligations to us.
   Senator Wayne Morse, in debate

May 18, 1963: A Diefenbaiter?
Adroit statecraft by the American State Department brought
down the bumbling, crypto anti-Yankee government of John
Diefenbaker . . . Mr. Diefenbaker took the bait nicely . . . and
Canadians turned their backs on him just as the State
Department knew they would. The American intervention was
coldly calculated to do precisely what it did – and it was a
brilliant success.
   Richard Starnes, Scripps-Howard columnist

January 21, 1964: Mais Non!
I gather they too, in Canada, have their difficulties
with minority populations, with the French provinces
actually talking of seceding from the Dominion.
Certainly nothing could conceivably come of this,
could it?
   Lady Bird Johnson, diary entry during her visit to
   Ottawa

February 20, 1964: What Marketing Hath Joined Together . . .
We are going to be forced by elementary business logic to act in
line with what we all recognize – that our two countries form a
natural market of magnificent size and potential, a market that
should not be broken in two by artificial political barriers.
   Lynn A. Townsend, President, Chrysler Corporation
   of America, in an Empire Club speech at Toronto

April 25, 1964: The Ultimate Logic
From the point of view of economic principles, there is no doubt that Canada and the United States could employ the resources of North America most efficiently by developing the continent as a single great market . . .

But no modern peoples are likely to permit their destinies to be shaped purely by economic facts. While both Canada and America have been moving towards commercial liberalization during the past thirty years . . . both have drawn back, for political reasons, from the ultimate logic of the single market.
George Ball, Undersecretary of State

June 16, 1964: On The Take
Americans like their kissin' cousins, the Canadians, a lot better than the Canadians like them. The reason is simple. We can take the Canadians or leave them alone. They have to take us.
Jenkin Lloyd Jones, Tulsa **Tribune**

March 4, 1965: Canada as a Revolutionary By-Product
It is sometimes argued that Canada is largely an American product. So she is, but in the same sense as Protestantism was a product of Catholicism. The first English-speaking Canadians were protestants against the American Revolution. They fled in fear and resentment. Slowly the fear has passed, but the resentment remains.
John MacCormac, former New York Times *correspondent in Ottawa, quoted in the* Baltimore Sun

May 21, 1965: A Paen of Praise
It may be trite, and some of our readers may react with a bored "ho hum" to this editorial, but we cannot resist the impulse to say again what a blessing it is to have such a neighbour as Canada on the North . . . It is rewarding in these troubled times to visit a country where there is a sympathy and understanding for what the United States is doing in the world. It is reassuring to discuss world problems with foreigners and not be subjected to hostile reactions. It is a pleasure to be able to argue with foreign nationals about the policies of both

countries and to do it in an atmosphere of goodwill . . . It is worth remembering this staunch, democratic, vigorous ally when we read about anti-Americanism elsewhere in the world.
Des Moines Register

June, 1965: Slow Americans, That's Us
If one were asked to describe a Canadian in the simplest and most succinct language, it would not be surprising to hear Americans characterize a Canadian as a "slow American."

Results of a study of US attitudes
towards Canada conducted by the Institute for
Analytical Research, Peekskill, New York

June 11, 1965: Bitching As A National Sport . . .
The favourite Canadian sport after hockey and contemplating the national navel is taking a dim view of the United States. The sidewalks in front of the Montreal and Toronto American consulates must be wearing out from repeated demonstrations by determined Canadian back-seat drivers of the North American juggernaut . . . Anti-Americanism is the one thing French and English Canadians have in common. I am convinced that if there had been no United States, Canada would have had to invent one.

Professor Mason Wade, University of
Rochester, New York

May 28, 1966: . . . On the Other Hand, We're Forthright
Canada, which boasts of the second highest living standard in the world, is not about to become "wholly American within a generation," as some economists have mentioned. The Canadians are much too individualistic to accept either our economic domination or our leadership in world affairs . . . It's good to have such friends in today's world, friends who do not hesitate to let you know where they stand and why.

John S. Knight, publisher of the Knight
newspapers, in a Halifax speech

October 15, 1966: Better Fed Than Red?

The fundamental reason Canada is selling wheat to the USSR is that it wants the money the Reds offer. They ease their consciences with the assertion that it would be un-Christian to let Communists go hungry and because trade might make the Communists less Communistic. . .This disturbing attitude, which is based on a naive reading of current history, should cause deep concern among both US citizens and more sophisticated Canadians. Yet the fact is that Canadian-Soviet ties may increase in the period ahead, with a consequent profound risk in North American well-being and security.

Anthony Harrigan in an American Security
Council newsletter

July 1, 1967: A Birthday Bouquet

It is this vast, rich land of opportunity, loosely joined, bilin-gual, with its immense prairies and forests, its mineral wealth, its frozen wastelands stretching far into the Arctic Circle, whose vigorous, enterprising people celebrate Canada's Centennial today.

New York Times *editorial*

July 23, 1967: Son of Reciprocity

With most countries in western Europe and North America now members of regional trade blocs, I think it is essential that we reconsider the feasibility of working toward regional free trade arrangements of our own. Thus I would urge [Congress] to take a fresh look at Canadian-US trade relations, with a view to establishing a Canadian-US free trade area.

David Rockefeller, president of the
Chase Manhattan bank, in Toronto

December, 1967: Anyway, Nobody Called Us Teacher's Pet

Our historians find it a bore.

We hardly ever mention it.

Frankly, it doesn't get hit very often. Every once in a while, you'll find a course.

It gets pretty sketchy after the War of 1812.

It's never taught separate from the British Empire.

We came very near to creating a course in it last year. But you'd have to develop student interest.

The role Canada plays is really not very much at all.

Canada's role is more or less consistent with our policies. I haven't really read that much about it.

Comments of US history teachers asked about
Canadian history during the eighty-second meeting
of the American Historical Association in Toronto

March 5, 1968: Undefended Border Strikes Again

The world can see by lifting up its eyes that two nations can live face to face across a thin line that you find only on a map, a line without fencing or armed guards, with absolutely no fear of each other, with respect for each other. Their border is an unfortified, heart-warming symbol of trust, co-operation and friendship; the symbol of a bond. Such friends can disagree without sacrificing the peace. That is the great gift of our border with Canada.

Senator Everett Dirksen, in the Senate

November 20, 1968: You've Got To Be Taut

When you do business with your relatives, it is always pretty complex. We can't get along without each other in business and we both want to be politically independent as pigs on ice. Sometimes the frustration of such an experience is too much for our Canadian relatives and their nerves get taut. . .On our part, it's easier, because we're so busy with other things we don't always notice what's going on. . .Canadians thought they were going to have a British form of government, American technology and French culture. They ended up with a French form of government, British technology and American culture.

William Armstrong, Associate Dean, Columbia University
School of International Affairs

122

December 13, 1971: Mary Hartman, Mary Hartman
In its relations with the United States these days, Canada feels a little bit like a woman having an affair with the big, rich man next door. She depends on him and he's a good provider, but he has a roving eye and a lot of other offers elsewhere.

James Reston, of the New York Times

1972: Access Makes The Heart Grow Fonder
Canada is a rich repository of natural resources vital to our economy now and certain to be even more so in the future. How much access we have to those resources – minerals, petroleum, natural gas, wood, and perhaps most important of all, water – will determine the shape of our economy, even our standard of living.

Richard J. Walton, foreword to Canada And The US

August 23, 1972: Don't Do Me Any Favours, Herman
The Canadians should understand that there are clear-cut alternatives [for US resource purchases], that they are not doing any favour to the US by selling them such things. Just the exact opposite is true. The customer does the favours. There is no point in Canadian nationalism. . . . But if you want nationalism, that's okay, it's as good as anything, as long as you are enjoying yourselves.

Herman Kahn, Director of the Hudson Institute, in an interview with the Toronto Star

November 2, 1974: This Land Is Posted
Canada – a kind of vast hunting preserve convenient to the United States.

Edmund Wilson, quoted in Saturday Review

November 2, 1974: Come Again?
In spite of Dave Barrett's visit and his kiss on her cheek, Ma Murray is particularly keen to get enough British Columbians off their butts to throw the Social Credit party out of office.

Frank Riley, in a special section on Canada, Saturday Review

Misconceptions

We Always Say Please
There is no rape in Canada, very little, anyway. You
know why? Because they electrocute the guy up there.
That cools the bastards out. It's okay by me.
High school student, Pittsburgh, Pennsylvania

Feel His Nose, I Think He's A Canadian
As far as I can make out from the people who come in here,
Canadians are just like anybody else, only colder.
Official greeter, Welcome Bureau,
La Crosse, Virginia

Tout le monde? Eh Bien, Presque Tout . . .
Canadians speak French, it's a fact. An American, if he speaks
French, you know he's a diplomat or highly educated or
something. It's not something a guy does, right? Well, we were
coming out of a movie one day and there was this guy on the
sidewalk jabbering away and I didn't know what he was
saying or anything, so my boyfriend says, "That's French, he's
speaking French." And this guy comes up, he starts jabbering
away, too, and gestures and everything and it turns out – my
boyfriend asked the second guy what was going on and it turns
out the first guy was lost, he was just looking for his hotel, and
he didn't speak any English. He was kind of a dark fellow,
from one of those places where they don't speak English. And
my boyfriend says "But how did you know to speak French?"
and the guy says, "Well, I'm a Canadian." I guess they all
speak French up there.
High school student, Nashville, Tennessee

124

Tundra And Lightning
I don't know. All I think of, I think of Canadians going to work every day, walking across the tundra. Cute.
Law student, Washington, DC

Yeah, But We Got No Panhandle
Canada is about the same size as Alaska, right?
Student, University of Hawaii, Honolulu

But No Man Is An Island
It's a very interesting place, we were there. Not every province is an island, but every island is a province.
Widow, Biloxi, Missouri

Not Only That, The Laundrymen Speak Chinese
The Canadians are among the most educated people in the world. I was stationed in Ottawa for a while, and you couldn't help but notice that even the hatcheck girls and cab drivers spoke French. We were very impressed.
Commercial attaché, Washington, DC

Not Foreign, Strange
When I was going for my fellowship, at the oral board they asked me what foreign countries I'd visited. I said "Canada," very proudly, and they laughed. To them, Canada wasn't a foreign country. The ignorance here is appalling.
Graduate student, University of Rochester, New York

State of Confusion, Of Course
What state is Baffin Island In?
Unemployed waiter, Waikiki, Oahu, Hawaii

That's Okay, We Like Your Queen, Rosalynn Carter
I think it's refreshing that your President has such a young wife. So pretty to look at.
Housewife, Mobile, Alabama

In A Barber Shop In East Holden, Maine
"Pardon me, but can you tell me anything about Canada, or Canadians?"
"Short hair."
"Anything else?"
"Nope."

That's OK, I Don't Care What You're Digging, Either
I don't know nothing about it, and I don't want to know nothing about it, and that's it.
Backhoe operator, Syracuse, New York

How We Treat Them

Good for Canada

My boy got his draft notice and said to hell with it and went up to Canada. He got a job up there, he's an English major, but he got a job working with crippled kids, for the government, not much money but he liked it. He couldn't come back here, of course, he's still on the indictment list as a deserter. He wasn't good enough for the US, but he was good enough for Canada, so now he's becoming a Canadian citizen. Good for him, and good for Canada, treating him right.

Pensioner, Washington, DC

Win A Few...

One time we were up in Muskoka – that's in Ontario – on a holiday, and the car broke down. We were driving along and the car suddenly stopped. So we pulled over off the road and just sort of sat there wondering what to do and along came a car and stopped right away. The man got out and asked us if anything was the matter and we explained, and he was real nice. He took Jim to a service station about ten miles away and insisted on coming back with the garageman, and took us over to his cottage and we had coffee and chatted with his wife while the car was being fixed.

Well, while Jim was gone with this man to the garage, there must have been half a dozen cars stopped to see what was the matter and the people would come and ask me if they could do anything, and I would say no, I was just waiting for my husband to come back with the garageman. But it really gave me a warm feeling. The way people stopped to see how you were, and why you were stopped. You wouldn't ever get that in the States. Here, they just drive right on by.

Housewife, Detroit, Michigan

127

... Lose A Few

I always heard Canadians were friendly people, but I'm not so sure. One time when we were up there on holiday – it was on that big highway between Toronto and Montreal, about the only really big highway you see up there – we ran out of gas. And believe me, the missus had something to say about that. Anyway, I pulled over to the side of the road and put a white hankie on the aerial and put the hood up to show people I was in trouble, and I stood there trying to thumb a lift.

I stood there for over three quarters of an hour, and not a single blessed person would help. They just kept going right on by. I don't know whether they thought I was Jack the Ripper or some kind of crook or what, but wasn't nobody going to stop and help us.

Finally, a cop come along, and he radioed to a station and the guy come out and soaked me eighteen bucks. What could I do? I don't believe people on this side of the border would leave a man stranded like that. Not where I come from.

Farmer, Cedar Rapids, Iowa

Can't Even Lug A Gun

We went up to the border once, but they wouldn't let my Dad through with his rifle and pistol, so we had to come back, 'cause he wouldn't go anywhere without a gun, he needs it for protection. Why would they do that to him?

Mechanic, Napa, California

Putting Up Barriers

We have property in Canada, and we received a notice telling us that if we sell it to another American, there's a tax. It's just a summer place, but I felt really offended, and I think it's a shame. Canadians have never been provincial before. A lot of Americans have Canadian relatives, and a lot of Canadians have American relatives. I think that kind of tax is deplorable, setting up barriers in a world where there are already too many.

Housewife, Grand Rapids, Michigan

128

Well, You Burned York

They came and burned the White House, you know. Of course it wasn't the White House then, it was the President's house. That was in the War of 1812. And it wasn't exactly Canadians, they were British troops mostly, I imagine, but it amounted to the same thing, the White House didn't know the difference.

Guide at the Lincoln Memorial, Washington, DC

Sing A Song of Syncrude

Canadians are very touchy right now, I don't know if it's a good time even to be talking about this, but as long as this is not for attribution, okay, I think it's a good thing to get some of these problems out in the open as long as it doesn't affect the company. We do a lot of business in Canada, I've just come back from a trip to Edmonton, and frankly, things are pretty rough up there. We sell a lot of supplies, things in the oil business and we've been up there for quite a while now on this Mackenzie Valley thing and then on this Syncrude deal, looking around, putting together a few things. At first, everything was just rosy, and we were heroes, Americans I mean. Then it wasn't so rosy and right now you'd think we were trying to steal the family jewels instead of do people a favour.

I tell you this for your own good, nothing personal. I think it's a matter of fact, you could look it up, that American money and American know-how is what built the oil industry in Canada. The stuff was there in the ground and nobody wanted to put the money in to get it out. That's a fact.

Then along came the Americans and you had Leduc and you had a big boom and everything was fine. Nobody was pissing on the Americans then. Then you went along and you had this nationalist business starting up, a few people who got it into their heads that the wicked Americans were stealing them blind, which was not the case. You had these people going around saying the oil should be kept in the ground, which is stupid on the face of it because as sure as God made little green apples somebody's going to come along with some new system, be it solar energy or nuclear energy or whatever and then what good is that oil going to be? It can sit there.

You had people saying save the environment, which is very true and I agree, but it is possible to get out the oil and not destroy the environment as everybody knows who has any idea about these things. I'm not saying you don't get problems, I'm saying those problems are part of progress and that's been true ever since the Industrial Revolution.

You had this situation with these nationalists running off at the mouth and the Alberta government started to cave in. The federal government wasn't much better, worse in fact. If you care to look at the speeches of Premier Lougheed of Alberta, you'll see what I mean. You can just see him start to swing. At first he was gung ho and let's get Syncrude going, and the Mackenzie Valley Pipeline, and then he started to slow down. A lot of companies put a lot of money into this thing, on good faith. They were willing to take a chance because they could see this big development coming, not just for Canada but for all of us because like it or not we're all in the same boat on this energy thing.

Anyway, Lougheed started to back off, and you had negotiations and negotiations and new meetings and the thing got so screwed up and turned around, God knows what's going to happen now.

The Mackenzie Valley thing is at a dead standstill while this commission goes around the North and says "Pardon me, but do you mind an oil pipeline in your backyard?" to every Indian and Eskimo, which we know what they are going to say – No, because that's what they've been told. And the people that put in the money, they don't know whether Syncrude is going to go ahead, or what, and on what terms, because there have been so many changes, there could be a lot more. And if you ask me, that's a hell of a way to treat people that just came in hoping to do something for Canada and maybe make a buck while they were at it.

Construction equipment salesman, Toledo, Ohio

After All We've Done For Canada . . .

The bastards put up the price of oil, and I don't think much of that. You expect the frigging Arabs to screw you, that's what they're for, but after all the things we've done for Canada I sure as Christ didn't expect to see them stick it to us on the oil prices. If you ask me, we shouldn't have taken that lying down.

Truck driver, Wheeling, West Virginia

Service Note
You can't get a glass of iced tea in Canada. Just getting an ice cube in your hotel is a major feat.
Store clerk, Augusta, Georgia

Where Did We Go Wrong?
A while ago they were anxious to have a larger population up there, they wanted people to come and live in Canada and they were thinking of growing. Now it turns out they don't want any Americans up there, I don't know what we did to deserve it.
Hardware merchant, Taos, New Mexico

The Saddest Thing
I'm very sad about the current state of Canadian-American relations. The government up there is putting all kinds of rules on that seemed to be aimed just at us. There's the law that says advertisers who put their money into *Reader's Digest* or *Time* can't deduct it from their taxes, there's the move against advertisers here in Buffalo beaming TV ads into the Canadian market. Well, maybe these things are necessary as the Canadians see it. You've got about $20 million in advertising beamed into Canada from here, and that's a lot of money. I don't know all the ins and outs of it, just what I read in the papers. What I read is that the old special relationship between Canada and the US is out of date, used up, and to me that's one of the saddest things in the world.
Trust company officer, Buffalo, New York

Not very grown up
Canadians seem to think they have a God-given right to comment in a derogatory way on every single thing that happens in this country, to criticize our president, our foreign policy, our trade policy, our system of justice and every other damn thing, but at the same time, any time an American hints that Canada might not be the best of all possible worlds, there is a stink from Ottawa to Kamloops, BC, and all the editorial writers get out their best adjectives to castigate us for interfering in your internal matters. Frankly, it's not a very grown-up attitude.
Department of Commerce officer, Washington, DC

The Greatest Bunch Of Whiners I Ever Saw

I was on the Canada Desk – the European desk, it was then – for some time, and you could see a very definite trend begin to develop over the years. For a while it was poor little Canada, and that was true, I'm not denying it. You weren't so poor compared to Lithuania, but you had some problems and a lot of your problems were with the US.

Then there was a change, quite a noticeable change, after about, say, 1965. Anybody who was following the trade figures could see that Canada was now doing well, and anybody who spent much time in Canada could see that your economy was going along like a house on fire. But the bitching didn't stop. Hell no, if anything, it got worse. This isn't something I have ever said to a Canadian diplomat, because it could cost me my job, but you are the greatest bunch of whiners I ever saw. Every time something goes wrong, it's the fault of the wicked Americans. But you aren't above pulling a fast one or two yourselves.

There is a strong feeling around here from time to time that Canada would like to solve its own problems at the expense of the United States. Take the Michelin tire deal. When the Michelin tire company was coming into Canada, there were terrific subsidies offered by the government of Nova Scotia and the DREE people [Department of Regional Economic Expansion]. That was because Michelin was going to provide a lot of jobs in the Maritimes, and God knows you need jobs in the Maritimes. We took the position that all the subsidies to Michelin were, in effect, a hidden export subsidy, which is illegal under the GATT [General Agreement on Tariffs and Trade]. We suspected that most of the tires were going to be shipped into the US, and we wanted a special import duty put on them, because of the subsidies.

Your people came down here and whined like hell. The tires weren't going to be produced for the US market, no way, they were going to be sold in Canada. That's what you said. Of course, it was nonsense. Back home, you were assuring the rubber companies in Ontario, who were having a fit because of the grants to a competitor, that all the rubber was going out of the country. Down here, you were saying it was all for the Canadian market.

As it turned out, of course, most of your tires were for export. You were using tax funds to subsidize a French company to come to Nova Scotia to invade our markets. And why? Because you needed jobs in eastern Canada. You were trying to solve your problem at our expense.

Frankly, I never thought much of that approach, and I don't see why Americans should give in to it.

Former desk officer, State Department, Washington, DC

We Put Up The Money That Defends Canada

Canada goes ahead and trades with Cuba, trades with China, trades with all these people, has everything its own way and then if we say anything, it's "Oh, the United States is a big bully," and, "Oh, the United States is being mean to us." Lot of crap. The fact is that the United States puts up the money that defends Canada, and if it weren't for that, anybody could come in and take over the place and probably would have. And what do we get in return? A lot of bellyaching. Frankly, it makes me sick.

Small businessman, Wilmington, Delaware

Versions
of History

Say It Isn't So, John A.
They don't have any heroes, and not much history.
History student, University of
Rochester, New York

Hero Story
Canadians are tough buggers, don't let anybody tell you
different. I met a lot of them Canadians overseas, in the war, and
they were no pantywaists. France, Italy, you ask anybody was
there about Canadians. Tough buggers. In Italy, up around
Naples or some damn place, we had a Canadian outfit not too far
from us and we got to see them off and on. They got into some
heavy going and they turned up one day with a bunch of German
prisoners. You could see them, from where we were camped, a lot
of Germans under guard. Then, one day they weren't there any
more. I knew there hadn't been any trucks come in or anything,
so I asked one of the Canadian guys and he kind of laughed and
said, "I don't know, Mac, I guess they got lost." Lost, hell, ask me
the Canadians shot the bastards. Good riddance, too. So don't
give me any crap about Canadians, they aren't the softies people
make them out to be.
Veteran at an army reunion convention, Pittsburgh

Another Scenario

This place used to be owned by the Canadians, did you know that? Not the Canadians, really, of course, but the British. Same thing. It's all back there in the museum; I went to look at it. I got nothing else to do. The British built a fort here and then the French took it over and then the British came back and the French wrecked the place. Right over there, not a hundred yards from where we're standing. Then there was the revolution, and it became American. It really makes you feel funny, thinking if things had gone different we'd all be Canadians, wouldn't we?

Unemployed welder, Fort Pitt Museum,
Pittsburgh, Pennsylvania

The Indian Factor

I don't think Canadians have any idea how lucky they are, the way they live. Here everybody is afraid all the time, you keep your door locked and bolted, you keep your car locked at all times, you wouldn't ever let a stranger into the house. There are people out there who would do terrible things to you, terrible. People have a party and they come in with guns and raid you, steal the money and rape you. It happens, I've heard of it happening. In Canada, there is none of that. If I had my way, there would be a spear on every wall, for protection, but Gerry won't let me. He keeps a gun, he says that's all you need. I say, get them first, if anybody's going to do something to you, if you're going to fight back, you better hurt him bad, right away, or it's going to be too late. Isn't that terrible? Isn't that a terrible way to talk? What makes Americans so violent, anyway, and Canadians not? I think it's history. You look back and you see the history, how it's different. Americans were so cruel to the Indians, cheated them, killed them, took away their lands, lied to them to get the land, just pushed them out. When the cavalry comes in, comes to the rescue, everybody cheers, isn't that right? It goes back to that, to guns and violence for settling everything, now it's built into the national character, we can't do anything about it, even if we think it's terrible. Canada is lucky that way. You didn't kill your Indians.

Housewife, Arlington, Virginia

The Aroostook War

I have a very high regard for Canadians. I read somewhere that there are more Franco-Canadians in this state and in Maine and New Hampshire than there are in the province of New Brunswick. I think it very likely. Thousands of Canadians came down here during the Depression, looking for work. There wasn't much more here than there was back home, but I guess just moving gave them a sense of doing something. Many came because they had relatives in the region, people who had come earlier, part of the natural flow down the eastern seaboard. A great many of them are Catholics, which is all right by me, I'm Catholic, too. I suspect that helped them to settle among the Irish Catholics of this state. You had the unifying link of Catholicism without the friction of the language question that you got up in places like Ottawa where the French and Irish Catholics clashed over the schools in the early 1900s, as I'm sure you know. Here English was the language of instruction, and that was that, so they got along.

So there is a long history here of friendship with the Canadians and it goes back and back. About the only serious problem I can think of goes back to around the time of the Aroostook War. That was a kind of comic-opera affair between Maine and New Brunswick. It was called a war, but as far as I know, nobody got killed, just a few heads broken. It was a war about timber cutting, and it turned on the problem of where the border between the US and Canada actually lay. I mean, were you cutting our timber, or were we stealing yours?

One of the principle characters, the way I remember it, was a man named Baker, an American. He was a heller for action, had what they used to call "a swaller for territory." He started to stir things up to get a declaration that his property was in the United States. He stuck up an American flag, and when somebody took it down, Baker beat the hell out of him. The New Brunswick men were cutting timber along the Aroostook River, and Maine sent along a posse of idiots like Baker, and the Canadian militia captured them and put them in jail, and then our side seized the Canadian warden, and it went on like that for a while with everybody hot and bothered. Then it was settled by the Webster-Ashburton Treaty, which you can look up in your history books, and you'll find that was in 1842. And when the border line was finally drawn, there was old Baker firmly on the Canadian side of the line. He stayed there, too, and settled down and for all I know became a model Canadian citizen.

I know Canadians don't like to be told that you're just like Americans, but I've always thought of old Baker, and the fact that around here when you draw a line on the ground, it really doesn't matter which side you end up on, the Canadian or the American.

Retired school teacher, Springfield, Massachusetts

Bullish On Canada

To me, Canada is a very distinct country with a heritage with strong European roots, probably stronger than in this country, with the French and British connections, and many other countries besides. Most of my friends and relatives from Czechoslovakia went to Canada and they're into egg grading and raising hops and most of them are doing far better than they would have done in Europe.

One hears of Canada as very like the United States, but I don't see it that way. Its history is different, its traditions are different, its culture is different, and being European, I can appreciate that. It's cosmopolitan, with large cities, but it's broad, and has lots of room. Canada is endowed with tremendous natural resources, which it is barely beginning to use, and so far it is underpopulated, and I think Canada is the land of the future that lives today. Brazil is the land of the future which hasn't accomplished much, but Canada has. I'm very bullish on Canada. If I weren't so happy living in the United States, I would be very happy to live in Canada.

Corporation executive, Cambridge, Massachusetts

Culture and Kulture

A Knock . . .
Canadian cooking is terrible, they have the thinnest cookbook in the world. Talking about Canadian cooking is like talking about Italian war heroes.
TV production assistant, New York City

. . .And A Boost
They make the best whisky in the world, better than Scotch.
Bartender, Fremont, Ohio

Must Be The Feet
I understand they grow terrific grapes up there around Niagara, but they turn them into the crappiest wine in the world.
Wine worker, French Camp, California

To Say Nothing of Tonto
Walter Pidgeon comes from Canada, and Glenn Ford, so I guess they have strong culture up there.
Retired Teacher, Palm Springs, California

GOING THROUGH THE RYE

What Else Is There?
Canadian whisky is good, Canadian weather is bad and the
Canada goose is a bird. That's the sum total of my knowledge.
  History student, University of Arizona, Tucson

Pilgrims
They got a place up there in Montreal, damnedest thing you
ever saw. It's a shrine of some sort on the mountain, brother
something, he was a religious fella did a lot of miracles.
Catholic fella. We went up there to see it, see this shrine. It's up
on the mountain and you can go there in a buggy. They've got
buggies and these French fellas drive them, real pleasant fellas
they are, too. You get there and there's these stairs, a big long
stairs goes up to the shrine and you see these people, Catholic
people, all going up to the shrine, up those stairs, and they stop
and pray on every stair. Every damn step, and there must be
hundreds of them. I guess it's from being Catholic, my wife
says they do it in Europe, too. We didn't go up, too damn
many stairs, we just went back to the hotel and had a drink
instead.
  Butcher, Montpelier, Vermont

139

A Kind Word For the CBC

God bless the CBC, which is what Canadian culture is all about. We have our antenna turned to Canada all the time, and we listen to Canadian radio, too. You get nothing in this country like the Canadian documentaries, you get nothing like Barbara Frum or Peter Gzowski. You would think Americans would learn from that, and support public broadcasting here, but it is still the poor relation. Canada's great.

Student, University of Buffalo, New York

Wet Blanket

My mother always told me Canadians made beautiful blankets. You should get a Canadian blanket, she used to say. They really know how to make blankets up there. Well, I've seen Canadian blankets, and they look just like American blankets to me.

Waitress, Minot, North Dakota

Gourmet Note

The food in Nova Scotia is terrible. The accommodation is so-so, but the food is just awful. Unless you like seafood.

Businessman, Dover, New Hampshire

Musical Appreciation

Canada produced Anne Murray, what more can I say? Fantastic!

Insurance salesman, Richmond, Virginia

Literary Conversation With An English Lit Major, UCLA

"I don't know what to think of a country where I've never heard of a single writer from there. I've heard of British writers and German writers and Russian writers and French writers and I even know of a Swiss writer, but I have never heard of a Canadian writer."

"How about Morley Callaghan?"

"Who?"

"You've never heard of Pierre Berton, or Farley Mowat, or Margaret Laurence?"

"Margaret Laurence is a South African. I've heard of her. She's a South African."

"She's a Canadian."

"Well, it shows. I thought she was a South African. It shows what I mean about Canada."

How They
Treat Us

We're Too Damn Polite
The way Canada is treated by this country is a disgrace, if you ask me. I don't know why we do it. The most short-sighted thing I ever heard of. Our best friends, our very best friends in the world live in Canada, just across they way, and we pay absolutely no attention to them, none. You never hear about Canada on TV, never see them in the papers unless it's something bad, Mad Killer Escapes or something like that. Very little attempt is made to understand Canada's problems, it's just taken for granted that whatever is good for the United States is good for Canada. And when you put that together with whatever is good for General Motors is good for the United States, you've really got something – whatever is good for General Motors is good for Canada.

You always hear about other countries. Right now, the papers, the weekend paper was full of Panama and all its problems and this business of renegotiating the Panama treaty. I agree with that, the treaty should be renegotiated. That thing was drawn up at a time when the United States was the bully-boy of the Western world. Well, those days are past. Uncle Sam has been behaving like a bully-boy in Canada for a good long time, but hardly a word of complaint do we hear. Is that because Canadians never complain? I don't believe it, don't believe it for a minute. If you were Peruvians, you'd nationalize an oil company or blow up a bridge or something, and then by God, the papers would be full of it. Canada is just too damn polite, if you ask me.

Retired economics teacher, Hyattsville, Maryland

A Near-beer Country
Most of your companies appear to be subsidiaries of American firms, most of what you do is determined by others. Even in foreign affairs, Canada spends all its time reacting to what other countries do, especially the US. There's a lot of complaining in Canada lately, about being pushed around by us; but we wouldn't do it if you didn't let us get away with it. In a way, Canada isn't a country at all, it's a near-country, like a near-beer.
    Auto union official, Detroit

Yes, Sir
Most Canadian people have more respect for authority than most Americans. They're very similar to Americans, but more polite. I think it's because the family is considerably more important to them, family life is very important in Canada, from what I saw. They're much more closely knit. I was stationed at the border across from Hanna, Manitoba, for seven years, and made lots of friends with Canadians, and that's what impressed me about them – they're polite and respect authority, at least the ones I've seen.
    Border patrol officer, Cuballo, New Mexico

How About A Boil?
Yes, of course, problems arise in our dealings with Canada from time to time, but we can always resolve them without too much trouble. After all, you don't operate on a pimple.
    Treasury Department officer, Washington, DC

Keep It Quiet
When that fellow Porter teed off, I was angry and resentful. Angry and resentful. [William Porter, in December, 1975, on the occasion of his departure as ambassador to Ottawa, gave a small party for some Canadian reporters and complained to them about the "deterioration" in Canada-US relations, most of which he blamed on Canadian nationalism.] It is seldom enough we get to hear about Canada down here, and the only thing that gets into the papers is this fellow complaining. I don't think that's at all right. We are good friends and neighbours, and there are ways

143

to settle these things without splashing it all over the papers. Even if everything Porter said was right, there are ways and ways of doing things. In the case of Canada, the way to do things is quietly.

Food industry lobbyist, Washington DC

Or How About Saying "Please"?
You want to know how to get the Secretary of State to go up and visit Ottawa? Have Quebec declare its independence, elect about a dozen Communists to the House of Commons and nationalize a couple of oil companies. I don't promise, but that should do it.

Legislative aide, Washington, DC

A Plug
They don't have troubles, not like here. They treat black folks right.

Washroom attendant, Washington, DC

All the Same
White's white. They all the same. It don't make no difference whether they're called Canadians or Americans, they're all racists.

City College student, Washington, DC

But Who Gets The Pillow?
If sleeping with an elephant is too uncomfortable for Canada, all you have to do is sleep a little further away from the elephant. The amount of American intrusion into the Canadian economy is something Canada determines, not the US.

Economics lecturer, Albuquerque, New Mexico

Cuba, Perhaps?

I mean, let's put this thing in perspective. We have got to get along with Canada, we've got to treat her right. She's our neighbour, our friend, our trading partner, has been for years. If we can't get along with Canada, for God's sake, who can we get along with?

Independent businessman, Pittsburgh

Harsh Words

Ever Ride The Subway?
I don't think I could go there, it's an awful lonesome place.
Retired teacher, New Orleans

Well, No, Not Really
Is Toronto near Vancouver?
Biology student, University of Hawaii, Honolulu

Yeller-bellies
They took in draft dodgers, yeller-bellies, and that weren't right.
Pensioner, Kearney, Nebraska

Just You Wait ...
As soon as the energy shortage got rough, they put the blocks to us. Our great and good friends in Canada, without so much as a word of consultation, put up the price of natural gas from $1 to $1.60 per thousand cubic feet, and they've boosted it since. They said it was because they could get a better price for it elsewhere, so that's what they had to charge us. What could we do? Some areas of the country, like Vermont, to name just one state, are almost totally dependent on the Canadian gas. So we just smiled and said okay, but to ourselves we said, "Okay, you bastards, just wait until you need something from us."
Federal Energy Administration worker, Washington, DC

How Are Things In Rankin Inlet?
We visited Canada for a week, up around Niagara Falls. Very
commercial. It was a great disappointment. We went all over
Canada and it was all very commercial.
Waitress, Louisville, Kentucky

Hey, Big Spender ...
Canadians seem to have a lot of money. They spend a lot when
they come in here, anyway.
Store owner, Minot, North Dakota

Well, Polar Bears, For One Thing ...
They were planning to hold our convention up in
Canada, but a bunch of us said what can you get
anywhere in Canada that you can't get better right
here? So we held the thing here.
Hardware supply salesman, Cortland, New York

The Ugly Canadians
As a matter of fact, the feeling about Canadians isn't too damn
friendly around here about now. A guy ran for office in this
county a while back on a straight anti-Canadian ticket, and he
damn near made it. I'd have voted for him, too, except he was a
damn fool.

You see, what's happening is that Canadians are coming down
here from British Columbia and buying up all the land. Then
they come down here and tell us what we're doing wrong. They
don't pay any attention to the speed limits, they just barrel along
the highway at any old speed and frankly, we resent it. Canadians
may have all the oil and gas in the world, but we don't. And that
55-mile-an-hour limit was put in for what seems to us a pretty
good reason and when some guy with a big car goes barrelling
past you at seventy or eighty miles an hour, you resent it. That's
only human nature. When's he's got a Canadian licence plate on,
you say, "What the hell?"

Canadians think of themselves as the world's nice guys, but
around here, you'd get some argument. This business of the land
is probably the major thing. I don't know whether it's because of
that Socialist government they had up in BC or the land freeze or

147

what, but this place is swarming with Canadians willing to pay top dollar for any recreational land. There's whole communities out here, for God's sake, where everybody stands up and salutes when they play "God Save The Queen." The result is that the local people can't get to the lakes, can't afford to buy the land because Canadians have driven up the price, and there's a real ugly feeling beginning to develop around here.

Businessman, Bellingham, Washington

On The Phone In Boothbay Harbor, Maine
"I want to place a call to Winnipeg, Manitoba, please."
"Manitoba, where's that?"
"It's in Canada."
"Well you can't expect me to know that. This is the United States."

Bugged by Smug
They complain about American ignorance of Canada, and it's true, but Canadians know very little about the people of the US. All they know is what they see on TV, and they believe it, every word. I'm always having to explain to my Canadian friends that my friends don't lock and bolt their doors every night, and they don't all carry guns. They think every place in America is like the New York they see on television. It isn't so. I lived in Boston, and nothing ever happened to me there; I went up to Ottawa, and a man exposed his penis to me on the street.

Teacher, Bennington, Vermont

What's In a Name?
What the hell would I know from Canada, this is America.

Clerk, Canadian Fur Store, Pittsburgh

An Exchange of Letters

Mr. John Chancellor,
NBC,
New York City
Dear Mr. Chancellor:

I hesitate to intrude on your busy day, but you cost me twenty-five cents, so we are out of the realms of diplomacy and into those of hard cash.

When we sat down to watch your three-hour special on foreign policy last night, my wife said she would bet me two bits Canada would not be mentioned, not even once. I told her, of course, that she was full of peach fuzz. Not only is Canada the single largest trading partner the US has, not only are we her closest friend and ally, but we are the beneficiaries, and victims, of a "special relationship" with the US. I pointed out that we were bound to make it, if only in the show's section on clichés. What is more, Canadian-American relations are under new, perhaps dangerous strain. Smart cookies like those guys at NBC, with their staffs of researchers, gaggles of assistants, prides of producers, wouldn't miss that, I said. Joan said uh-huh, and where was the two bits? I put it up.

Three hours later, I passed it over. I thought you were going to slip us in, after maybe Brazil or Belgium, or where you got talking about vital imports, or multi-nationals. When Switzerland made it, then Yugoslavia, Mexico, Taiwan and Jamaica, I was sure we were next. Nope. You gave the closest-friends-and-allies cliché to Japan, Western Europe and Israel, one of the neatest parlays of all time, and you gave the "special relationship" to Japan, may she wear it proudly.

Poorer and wiser now, I have a couple of questions to ask, not as a sorehead, but as a journalist, and the loser of two bits. No big deal, just a scrawled yes or no will do:

    (a) In production meetings, was Canada mentioned and rejected, or
    (b) Did you forget about us?
    (c) Are we not a foreign country?
    (d) Would it help if we blew up the Peace Bridge?

William Porter, your late ambassador to Ottawa, says Canadian-American relations are "deteriorating," and I think he has the right dope. The implications are profound, not only for us, but for you. Please look again.

Walter Stewart

Mr. Walter Stewart,
Maclean's Magazine,
Washington, D.C.
Dear Mr. Stewart:

Your letter to Mr. Chancellor was referred to me because I produced the program on Foreign Policy.

I enjoyed your letter despite its critical tone concerning our non-coverage of Canada. In the interests of peace and friendship between our two countries, I've attached a twenty-five cent coin [American] to this letter since I did not want you to be out any cash because we failed to mention Canada in the show.

Answering your questions in the order they were given:
   (a) Canada was mentioned very often in our production meetings;
   (b) We didn't forget about you;
   (c) Canada is a foreign country;
   (d) Please don't blow up the Peace Bridge.

One of our first considerations in researching this show was the treatment of Canada. I wanted very much to include the relations with your country in the program, including the recent deterioration as Mr. Porter called it, but we finally decided that Canada would have to be left out because of time considerations. You must admit it was a tight show. There were three or four other countries we had to leave out, one of them despite the fact that we filmed there for ten days – that was the Philippines, another old and close friend. My decision was based on the fact that though Canada and the United States may have some problems in their diplomatic relations, these problems are nothing as compared with the difficulties the United States is experiencing in relation to the rest of the world. I think you will agree to that. So we decided that our good friends to the North would have to be covered elsewhere at another time, perhaps in the way we did four or five years ago when we produced and aired two one-hour programs about your country.

Thanks for your letter and for bringing up this point. I really expected a lot more letters about this than we have actually received, but maybe more will be coming in in the next batch.

Sincerely yours,
Dan O'Connor,
Executive Producer, NBC

Some Presidential Pronounce- ments

George Washington, 1775
As the contempt of the religion of a country by ridiculing any of its ceremonies, or affronting its ministers or votaries, has ever been deeply resented, you are to be particularly careful to restrain every officer from such imprudence and folly, and to punish every instance of it. On the other hand, as far as lies in your power, you are to protect and support the free exercise of the religion of the country, and the undisturbed enjoyment of the rights of conscience in religious matters, with your utmost influence and authority.

*from Washington's Instructions to Benedict
Arnold in the attack on Quebec*

James Madison (date uncertain)
I have another idea by which you can make sure of the safety of Canada and it will be less costly. Eliminate all fortifications on the border. It will be cheaper, and without guns neither of us will be able to attack one another, except maybe to throw rocks.

from a private letter

James Monroe, December 2, 1826
That the American continents, by the free and independent condition which they have assumed and maintained, are henceforth not to be considered as subjects for future colonization by any European powers.

from his message to Congress. This became known as the Monroe Doctrine.

Andrew Johnson, 1867
The acquisition and incorporation into our Federal Union of the several adjacent and continental and insular communities [is necessary] as speedily as can be done peacefully, lawfully and without any violation of natural justice, faith or honour. Foreign possession or control of those communities has hindered the growth and impaired the influence of the United States.

Ulysses S. Grant, 1870

The Colonial authority known as the Dominion of Canada . . .
this semi-independent but irresponsible agent has exercised its
delegated powers in an unfriendly way.

Theodore Roosevelt, 1895

**Let the fight come if it must; I don't care whether our
sea coast cities are bombarded or not; we would take
Canada.**

*Roosevelt was sore about the Alaska boundary
dispute, in which he claimed Canada behaved with
"bumptious truculence."*

William Howard Taft, 1911

Now is the accepted time. Canada is at the parting of the ways.
Shall she be an isolated country, as much separated from us as
if she were across the ocean, or shall her people and our people
profit by the proximity that our geography furnishes and
stimulate the trade across the border that nothing but a useless,
illogical and unnecessary tariff wall created?

Warren Harding, 1923

I find that, almost unconsciously, I am speaking of our two
countries in the singular when perhaps I should be more
painstaking to keep them where they belong, in the plural. But I
feel no need to apologize. You understand as well as I that I speak
in no political sense. The ancient bugaboo of the United States
scheming to annex Canada disappeared from all our minds years
and years ago. Heaven knows we have all we can manage now,
and room enough, too . . . No, let us go our own gaits along
parallel roads, you helping us and we helping you. So long as
each country maintains its independence, and both recognize
their interdependence, those paths can not fail to be highways of
progress and prosperity.

in Stanley Park, Vancouver

Herbert Hoover, 1931

I have been very glad to welcome today the Canadian Premier [R. B. Bennett] upon his informal visit to Washington. We have no formal matters under discussion. We are mutually interested in the common welfare of our peoples. Informal conversations on problems of the future always lead to better understanding.

Franklin Delano Roosevelt, 1936

While I was on my cruise I read in a newspaper that I was to be received with all the honours customarily rendered to a foreign ruler.

Your Excellency, I am grateful for the honours; but something within me rebelled at that word "foreign." I say this because when I have been in Canada I have never heard a Canadian refer to an American as a "foreigner." He is just an "American." And, in the same way, in the United States, Canadians are not "foreigners," they are "Canadians."

That simple little distinction illustrates to me better than anything else the relationship between our two countries. On both sides of the line we are so accustomed to an undefended border three thousand miles long that we are inclined perhaps to minimize its vast importance, not only to our own continuing relations, but also to the example which it sets to other nations of the world.

Quebec City speech. Note how the undefended border keeps changing its size, anywhere from 3,000 to 4,500 miles long. It is, in fact, 3,987 miles.

FDR, 1938

The Dominion of Canada is part of the sisterhood of the British Empire. I give you the assurance that the people of the United States will not stand idly by if domination of Canadian soil is threatened by any other Empire.

speech at Kingston, Ontario

Harry Truman, 1947

Canada's eminent position today is a tribute to the patience, tolerance, and strength of character of her people, of both French and British strains. For Canada is enriched by the heritage of France as well as of Britain, and Quebec has imparted the vitality of spirit itself to Canada. Canada's notable achievement of national unity and progress through accommodation, moderation and forebearance can be studied with profit by her sister nations.

Much the same qualities have been employed, with like success, in your relations with the United States. Perhaps I should say "your foreign relations with the United States," but the word "foreign" seems strangely out of place. Canada and the United States have reached the point where we no longer think of each other as "foreign" countries.

Address to Parliament, Ottawa

Truman, 1949

The President:
I have invited the Prime Minister of Canada to visit Washington on February 12. He has accepted the invitation and it is expected he will arrive in Washington on the evening of February 11 and will remain probably for two days. The Prime Minister's acceptance of the invitation will permit us to renew his acquaintance – I became very well acquainted with him November 15, 1948 – after having served first as Minister of Justice and then as Secretary of State for External Affairs since 1941 [sic. Actually, St. Laurent was Secretary of State for External Affairs only from 1946 to 1948]. This will be the Prime Minister's first trip to the United States since he assumed his duties as Prime Minister. I meant to say that I am acquainted with him on my trip up – my visit to Canada. That was the first time I had met him, and I am inviting him down here for the purposes of becoming better acquainted with the Prime Minister of our neighbour.

Question:
For bulletin purposes, what's his name?

The President:
I very carefully was trying to avoid it, because I don't know how to pronounce it: Louis St. Laurent – L-a-u-r-e-n-t – I don't know how to pronounce it.

Press conference, Washington, DC

Dwight D. Eisenhower, 1953
You people here have a great country with great possibilities, so don't let them ruin your water. We have ruined ours in the States with our growth of population so that the great, beautiful rivers that flow into the Atlantic and down through the Mississippi Valley are contaminated. You should remember this, that really great water is one of your greatest assets. But when you've got a lot of it, you don't think about it.

in conversation with Ontario Premier Leslie Frost

Eisenhower, 1958
I am confident that if there are some defects in this investment process, ways will be found to correct them because that is in the interests of both our countries.

Press conference, Ottawa

John F. Kennedy, 1961
We share common values from the past, a common defence line at present, and common aspirations for the future, and indeed the future of all mankind.

Geography has made us neighbours, history has made us friends. Economics has made us partners. And necessity has made us allies. Those whom nature hath joined together, let no man put asunder.

Address to Parliament, Ottawa

Lyndon Baines Johnson, 1967
You have focussed the eyes of the world on the theme of your exhibition: Man And His World. We hope that, among other lessons to be learned here, will be this: that proud and independent peoples can live peacefully side by side, can live in peace and partnership as good neighbours, that they need not waste their substance and destroy their dreams with useless quarrels and senseless, unconstructive conflict.

We of the United States consider ourselves blessed. We have much to give thanks for. But the gift of Providence that we really cherish is that we were given as our neighbours on this great, wonderful continent, the people and the nation of Canada.

at EXPO '67

Johnson, 1971
Canada is such a good neighbour that our problems are kind of like a problem in the home town.
press conference, Washington, DC

Richard M. Nixon, 1972
I would have to say quite candidly that we have had very little success to date in our negotiations with our Canadian friends, which shows, incidentally, that sometimes you have more problems negotiating with your friends than you do with your adversaries.

press conference, Washington, DC

Nixon, 1972
It is time for Canadians and Americans to move beyond the sentimental rhetoric of the past. It is time for us to recognize that we have very separate identities; that we have significant differences; and that nobody's interests are furthered when these realities are obscured.

Our peaceful borders and our peaceful history are important symbols, to be sure. What they symbolize, however, is the spirit of respect and restraint which allows us to co-operate despite our differences in ways which help us both. American policy towards Canada is rooted in that spirit. Our policy toward Canada reflects the new approach we are taking in all of our foreign relations, an approach which has been called the Nixon Doctrine. That doctrine rests on the premise that mature partners must have autonomous, independent policies; each nation must decide the requirements of its own security; each nation must determine the path of its own progress.

address to Parliament

Gerald R. Ford, 1974
We in the United States know no other country where the United States has some four thousand or five thousand miles of border, when you consider that on the north and south, and also Alaska. And so there is a great reason for us to have a rapport and the

particular affection, people to people and country to country.

And I might say the first trip that I ever took out of the United States – I was quite young and quite thrilled – was the trip I took from Detroit to Windsor [Laughter].

They didn't preclude me from going to Windsor, and I had no trouble getting back [Laughter].

But that was a thrill to me, and it was my first trip out of the country and to a foreign country.

But my memories of that trip left me with a great remembrance of the relationship that our country has with yours. The truth is, of course, good friends often have many differences, and among friends differences fortunately can be better debated or discussed than they can when a different relationship exists.

toast at an Ottawa state dinner